Europe:
variations on a theme
of racism

Our special thanks to Hilary Arnott, Paul Bourne, Paul Gordon, Theo Itten, Cathie Lloyd, Danny Reilly, Lucien Senna and Frances Webber for their help with this issue.

© Institute of Race Relations 1991
ISBN 0 8500 1 037
Cover design by Arefin & Arefin
Typeset by Spencers (TU), 1-5 Clerkenwell Road, London EC1
Printed by the Russell Press, Gamble Street, Nottingham

RACE & CLASS

A JOURNAL FOR BLACK AND THIRD WORLD LIBERATION

Volume 32   January-March 1991   Number 3

Europe: variations on a theme of racism

ISSN 0306 3965

Editorial

'The problem for an open Europe', predicted this journal in 1988, 'is how to close it – against immigrants and refugees from the Third World.' Today, the structures for that closure are being set in place in the informal meetings of the Trevi group of ministers and police chiefs and the discussions of the inter-state treaty makers of Schengen. And, as before, the danger for democratic government, for accountable administration, shows itself in the erosion of the rights of some of its citizens and, therefore, for all of its citizens. For although Trevi is meant to be addressing the problem of terrorists and drug-runners and Schengen the problem of illegal immigrants and refugees, a common culture of European racism, which defines all Third World people as immigrants and refugees, and all immigrants and refugees as terrorists and drug-runners, will not be able to tell a citizen from an immigrant or an immigrant from a refugee, let alone one black from another. They all carry their passports on their faces.

And it is these aspects of the emergence of an institutionalised racism on a pan-European basis, fomenting and fomented by popular racism, that portend the drift towards an authoritarian European state.

To understand that, however, one has to understand the way that the different types of European racism have taken shape in the crucible of their particular national histories. Thus, where German racism would appear to stem directly from the aggregation of one *Volk* into a nation exclusive of all other *Volk*, French racism seems to have taken shape at the point where the Enlightenment, carrying the nation state in its arms, stubbed its toe against the colonies. Unlike Britain* which treated its colonies as peoples apart, to be acculturated only to be exploited, France saw the cultural assimilation of its subject peoples into a greater France as the burden of its Enlightenment. Where British racism was driven by the economic imperatives of the industrial revolution, French racism was driven by the cultural imperatives of the Enlightenment. Both racisms, however, were imbricated in the creation of the nation state. German racism, on the other hand, formed the very basis of that creation.

While these same processes of industrialisation and nation-building – with, of course, their different time-spans and their differential colonial encounters – appear to have shaped the national racisms of Europe, it was their need for cheap labour in the period of post-war

---

* We have not dealt with Britain in this issue as it has been widely covered in previous issues of *Race & Class*.

reconstruction that gave these racisms their particular point and purpose. Invariably, such labour came from either the colonies and ex-colonies of the Third World or from the then poor south of Europe, and were 'saddled' with different cultures, different colours, different creeds. What Europe wanted, though, was the labour not the labourer – and towards that end racism was a ready instrument.

But, with the passing of industrial society, that labour is no longer needed. The problem for European governments now is how to settle the labour that refuses to go back whilst evolving, at the same time, a common policy that will keep out any further intake of labour in the form of refugees and asylum-seekers. And yet, it is precisely such peripatetic migrants who form the ideal workforce, flexible and ad hoc, required by the manufacturing and service sectors of post-industrial society. Hence these governments are faced with two sets of contradictions. On the one hand, they are compelled, as a part of the tidying-up process for the new open Europe, to regularise the status of long-standing 'immigrants', but risk the danger of being thrown out of power by the popular racism that they themselves have engineered. On the other hand, they want to appease their racist constituencies by keeping out Third World migrants and refugees, but run the risk of undermining the black economy and the increased prosperity it brings.

Nor is it a viable policy to require that late-comers to the European economic miracle like Spain which need cheap migrant labour for their 'take-off', and the agricultural sectors of countries like Italy which can no longer find seasonal labour from within their own workforces, should seal tight their frontiers for the greater benefit of their more prosperous partners.

And then there is the problem of a falling and aging European population, particularly in the Scandinavian countries, and a growing anxiety about who is to do the work.

Already the cracks are beginning to show in the battlements of Fortress Europe even as its foundations are being threatened by the revolts of the new natives in Lyon and Lesjöfors.

A. Sivanandan

Myths and realities

JAN NEDERVEEN PIETERSE

Fictions of Europe*

'European culture'

It is not difficult to find a definition of 'European culture'. For instance:

> What determines and characterises European culture? . . . Europe is formed by the . . . community of nations which are largely characterised by the inherited civilisation whose most important sources are: the Judaeo-Christian religion, the Greek-Hellenistic ideas in the fields of government, philosophy, arts and science, and finally, the Roman views concerning law.[1]

This is a definition so average that it is almost official. In fact, it is official, because it is given by the Netherlands Ambassador for International Cultural Cooperation, Mr M. Mourik. We are taken past the familiar stations of Europe: Greece – Rome – Christianity. This is a well-known entity in the United States also, where it is often referred to as 'western civilisation', which may be summed up as 'from Plato to Nato'.[2]

This is the usual façade of Europe, so familiar that it is boring. This is the Europe that is now being resurrected in the discourses of the official magisters of culture. The problem, however, is not just that it is boring. The problem is that, in addition to being chauvinistic, elitist, pernicious and alienating, it is wrong.

Jan Nederveen Pieterse is author of *Empire and Emancipation: power and liberation on a world scale* (London, Pluto, 1989).
*Part of the revised text of a lecture given at the Yorkshire Arts Council in Bradford, November 1990. Part two, not included here, is called 'Scratching the Surface: multicultural Europe'.

Race & Class, 32(3), 1991

It is wrong as regards the origins of European culture; it is wrong in so representing European culture that European regional cultures and subcultures are overlooked; it is wrong in representing elite culture as culture *tout court* and in denying popular culture; it is wrong in defining European culture in terms of the past ('inherited civilisation') and in totally ignoring Europe's contemporary multicultural realities.

This old culture is presently being revived in the context of the 'new Europe'. Many of the political and economic negotiations and virtually all of the debate on culture focus on *Europe and the nations*. The usual questions are whether the Europe of '1992' will be dominated by the largest national European cultures, Germany and France. What about Britain? What about the identities of the smaller European cultures? What about central Europe, Mitteleuropa? Will European cultures be steamrollered into a continent-wide pattern of uniformity, propelled by market forces and media magnates and directives from a few Europe metropoles?

The continent that pioneered nationalism pioneers the transcendence of nationalism, and in this context these questions are very meaningful. Yet, this is essentially a discussion about 'Europe and Europe'. There is another question on the horizon which is both larger and potentially more incisive in its implications, and that is *Europe and the continents*. This is infrequently talked about, except in the context of decolonisation and the critique of eurocentrism, topics which are not particularly high on the agenda.

We are living in a post-imperial Europe which still maintains an imperial culture. Official European culture, reproduced in declarations, textbooks, media programmes, continues to be the culture of imperial Europe.

Another issue is that Europe, from the point of view of the many migrants in Europe of non-European origin, is now a New World, yet its self-image, its dominant culture, is still that of an Old World – that is, a world from which people emigrate.

Certain key experiences are missing from this new old European culture: the experience of decolonisation, of migrations, post-imperial ('we are here because you were there') and otherwise, and of globalisation.

Walk in any street of any European city and ask yourself – is this 'European culture'? Is this 'Greece – Rome – and Judaeo-Christianity'? Ask contemporary citizens of Europe about their ancestors, their origins – how many of you hail from non-European worlds? Or, to use nineteenth-century racist language, how many of you are half-caste? How many of you were never represented in this elite European project in the first place – as members of the working class or living in the countryside, or in regional cultures such as the 'Celtic fringe'?

What is being recycled as 'European culture' is nineteenth-century elite imperial myth-formation. Is it not high time then to open up the imperial façade of European culture, to place it under an X-ray and ask, what here is really Europe and what is not?

Fortress Europe

Europe 1992 means that, as internal borders become lower, the external borders become higher, both in terms of the 'Zollverein Europe' of the internal market and in terms of 'European identity'. Concretely, it refers to the plans for a 'European visum' and to the Schengen Accord, which is to regulate immigration and asylum on a European basis.

Each European country thereby assumes a double identity, national and as member of a United States of Europe, each a gateway towards, or a ramparts of the European world. As the physical frontier with Africa and the Middle East, Mediterranean Europe occupies a special place in this constellation. There are writings on the wall.

Spain, Portugal and Greece have recently become immigration countries – now more people come from the south than leave for the north. Italy had already held this status for some time. Thus, the Italian and French patterns of racism and racial attacks on minorities of non-European origin, mainly from North and West Africa, may be becoming a Mediterranean pattern. Spanish sociologist Alberto Moncada speaks of 'Spain functioning as a southern European police over the human mass from the Maghreb and Latin America'.[3] In news reports, Greece and also Bulgaria are already talked about as 'frontline states with fundamentalist Islam'.

What is developing in these areas is a European Mexico syndrome – a border-zone where economic, political, cultural, religious and demographic differences accumulate to create a gap between worlds, a zone of confrontation. Like Hong Kong, Europe will, and indeed already does, face refugees, boat people, and police hunting for illegal foreigners.[4]

NATO is also shifting its sights towards the south.[5] With the cold war past, this is where the 'new enemy' lurks. 'Islamic fundamentalism', poverty and high population growth are identified as the main problems in classified and not-so-classified documents. Over recent years, we have seen the enemy images shifting and 'new Hitlers' paraded on the front pages – Arafat, Khadafi, Khomeini, Assad, and now Saddam Hussein.

Thus, Fortress Europe is becoming a reality. The situation is primarily identified as a security problem, although it is also, secondarily, acknowledged as an economic and humanitarian problem.

Europe's historic frontier of confrontation with the world of Islam is being reactivated. The question of Europe and the south, Africa, Asia and Latin America, is acquiring new dimensions. We may sum up this set of problems as: *Europe and the continents*.

These problems also reflect on migrants of non-European origin within Europe, so they also run *through* Europe. We may sum up this question as: *Europe and the minorities*. Thus, the problems of Europe and the continents are reproduced locally throughout Europe, interacting with the problem of Europe and the minorities. Local frontiers, of status and neighbourhood, colour and education, intersect with global frontiers. How minorities of non-European origin are viewed is affected by how Europe views itself in relation to the continents.

The prospect is that of Europe as a fort, with the Straits of Gibraltar and the Bosphorus for moats, and parts of the Third World as hinterlands, optional labour reserves. Gradually, a discreet neo-Malthusianism is becoming a way of thinking about Africa in particular: famine and starvation as the means of re-establishing equilibrium between population and resources.

The inauguration of 'Europe 1992' will coincide with the 1992 Columbus celebrations in Spain and Portugal and the Americas – 500 years since the Old World spawned the New World, 500 years of modernisation, 500 years to contemplate the paradoxes of progress . . . In Spain and Portugal, this will be an occasion to erect monuments to commemorate the 'Discoveries' and to celebrate the Conquista, thereby reaffirming and reproducing in their claim to fame the very dualism of the Americas, where Columbus Day is a day of celebration for Europeans and a day of mourning for native Americans.

European identity is no longer an imperial, expansionist identity in the old sense. The era of imperialism is past. The era of decolonisation is past and Third Worldism is no longer à la mode. European chauvinism now is prosperous, complacent, aloof. Fortress Europe, in its cultural uniform, is not expansionist but critical.

Many 'progressives', intellectuals and left-wing people included, share this kind of definition of the situation. Europe is their castle. Europe is the fortress of their mind. As much as they identify with the Europe of the Enlightenment, they abhor 'Islamic fundamentalism', and, since 'Third Worldism' is out of fashion, they look down, if they look at all, on the poor in the Third World, and find shelter in a self-image of Europe as a world of modernity. The discourse of post-modernism, busy critiquing modernity, turns its back on the 'pre-modern' world.

This situation is an open door to the European Right, culture-baiting minorities as 'aliens'. This creates the danger of a new European consensus of exclusion, a right-to-centre political and cultural coalition that may turn Europe into a complacent shelter of conservatism – in the name of Enlightenment.

One of the European projects waiting in the wings is that of a Europe-wide coalition of right-wing parties, a continental chain of 'national fronts'. It is ironical to realise that, for all their 'national' posturing, several of these organisations are being funded and supported from foreign sources, ranging from American right-wing foundations to the Unification Church of Rev Moon.

The deconstruction of Europe

Rather than recycling the illusions of imperial Europe, we should address and welcome the multicultural realities and opportunities of post-imperial Europe. Re-creating Europe in '1992' means to relocate Europe's place in world history, in terms of the real relationship between Europe and the continents and not according to the great walls of empire.

The familiar stations of Europe are: Greece – Rome – Christendom – Renaissance – Enlightenment – industrialisation – colonialism. The two main definitions of European identity derived from this are, in shorthand, Christianity and the Enlightenment.

From Santiago de Compostella, Pope John Paul II calls out to a 'Christian Europe'. This historical field mattered to Catholic states-men Schuman, Adenauer, de Gasperi, who came together for the Treaty of Rome in 1956. The notion of Christian Europe matters to Christian Democrats and to many on the Right, from Otto von Habsburg to Jean Marie le Pen.[6]

There is no question that the histories of Europe and Christianity are interwoven. Yet, indeed, there are many problems with defining European identity in terms of Christianity. What about the Renaissance, the humanists, the anticlericals, the Enlightenment? And what about the great schisms in Christianity – between Greek and Latin Christianity, between Constantinople and Rome, between Europe east and west, and between Roman Catholicism and Pro-testantism, between Europe south and north? Indeed, Christianity is Asian in origin, and on many medieval maps we find Jerusalem depicted as the centre of the world, an Asian site as the centre of the Christian world – this is the dominant depiction on *mappae mundi* from the seventh to the thirteenth centuries and occurs frequently on maps from 1200 to 1500.

Much more pervasive and more formidable as a definition of Europe is the legacy of the Renaissance/Enlightenment. The charac-teristic feature of the Europe of the Enlightenment, as Jack Liveley has argued, is the Enlightenment itself: European identity was discovered 'in the modernity of Europe'.

> The European personality was distinct and its role was unique, not because its traditionally rooted society marked it out from other cultures, but because it had moved sufficiently far along a path of development to serve as an example for the rest of humanity. The emphasis was now on time rather than space, promise rather than achievement, the future rather than the past . . . Moreover . . . the modernity of Europe consisted in the Enlightenment itself.[7]

Europe equals modernity, or the critical spirit, its attitude of self-criticism, its tolerance and openness to other views. From Kant to Raymond Aron, this is a recurrent theme.

It relates closely to another European topos: the 'autonomy of the spirit' as a European characteristic, the tension and friction between faith and reason, the aversion to dogma. This is Nietzsche's tradition of the free thinkers, the *libres penseurs*.

This, in turn, overlaps with a discourse which finds the specificity of Europe in the autonomy of its cities, hence the development of its burghers, its citizens and, over time, civil society.

Again we hear the echo of a classic theme: Europe as the land of liberty, as against Asia, the land of despotism and oppression – in a word, oriental despotism and occidental liberty. This is a thesis that harks back to the Greeks: to the east in Persia, despotism; to the north in Europe, the free barbarians; and in the middle, Greece, that is civilisation.

These overtones – autonomy, liberty – still play a part in Europe's self-definition but drawn into the background since the experiences with Nazism, fascism, European totalitarianism. The keynote in the self-assessments of Europe remains that of modernity. That is essentially the Europe of the Enlightenment, also as the dapper antidote to totalitarian Europe.

This is the most prominent rhetoric of difference between Europe and non-European worlds, in particular, between Europe and the world of Islam – the common European interpretation of 'fundamentalist Islam' is as a revolt against modernity (that is, against Europe), a countermodernisation and the International of '*Unvernunft*'.[8]

'Identity' implies a relationship to what is different and thus a statement of boundaries. Both these European identities – Christianity and the Enlightenment – are such statements of boundaries, border flags which serve as internal as much as external boundaries – protection from the 'barbarians' both within and outside the gates. They are projects rather than realities, mirrors of power and rhetorics of control.

European paradoxes

Why deconstruct Europe? It's not fair. It's hardly been constructed. Americans would say the same thing, why deconstruct Europe? We like Europe, it means a lot to us, it is the prototype of Disneyland.

It is true that European identity is weak. First, because Europeanism is recent. It dates, by and large, from after 1700. Before that, Christendom was the predominant identity. The humanists of the Renaissance looked towards Greece and Rome as the centres of culture. Moreover, until 1683 when the Turks stood before Vienna, Europe was still under threat from the east.

Second, European development has not known a single centre. There has been a continual shift of centres, and with the centre also the peripheries shifted. The Renaissance, the Enlightenment and French Revolution, industrialisation and colonial expansion, unfolded in different parts of Europe and spread in different directions. There was never a centre which embodied European identity.

Third, from 1700, European development has taken place by means of single rival states. Already, from the sixteenth century, Europe existed in the form of a 'European balance of power', that is as a polycentric world. From 1700, the keynote of political development were the different monarchies, while from 1800, the keynote of development was *national* development.

Also, outward expansion was undertaken by single rival states. Europe's 'new imperialism' of the late nineteenth century and the scramble for Africa was a preemptive imperialism – both in concert with European competitors and aiming to outmanoeuvre them. This is one of the paradoxes of European imperialism: it implied and brought forth both European unity (as in the Berlin Conference on the division of Africa) and European divisions.

Another paradox. The backdrop to nineteenth-century European expansion in Asia and Africa was a concept of 'European civilisation'. This was implied in the '*mission civilisatrice*', even if this was executed primarily by means of national missions. It correlated with racial thinking. 'European civilisation' made for a certain affinity among Europeans of different countries even while they were rivals for overseas territory and influence. This European civilisation, the bedrock of European superiority and arrogance, received a deadly blow with the First World War. The long conflict from 1914 to 1945 shook the foundations of Europe's overseas imperialism and ushered in the era of decolonisation.

Then 'Europe' was born – born out of the contraction of empire: thrown back upon themselves the European nations began to discover each other. 'Europe' was born in the shadow of the superpowers, not as the world's Queen, as she had been in eurocentric iconography since the sixteenth century, but merely as a buffer zone between the superpowers. Now, the superpowers themselves are waning and new centres are emerging.

References

1   M. Mourik, 'European cultural co-operation', in A. Rijksbaron, W.H. Roobol, M. Weisglas (eds), *Europe from a cultural perspective'. historiography and perceptions* (The Hague, 1987), p. 19.
2   Elissa McBride, 'Western Civilisation: From Plato to Nato', *The Activist* (No. 21, summer 1988), p. 7.
3   Information Bulletin XIIth World Congress of Sociology, Madrid, July 1990, No 1.
4   Plans are underway to 'manage' and control this problem zone. Spain, France, Italy and Portugal seek the establishment of a Conference for Security and Cooperation in the Mediterranean, a 'Mediterranean Helsinki', modelled on the European Conference for Security and Cooperation. Already they have established a Forum for Regional Cooperation in the Mediterranean, together with Morocco, Algeria, Tunisia, Libya and Mauretania – five countries united in the Arab Maghreb Union. *Volkskrant* (4 August 1990).
5   Mariano Aguirre, 'Looking Southwards', in Dan Smith (ed.) *European security in the 1990s* (London, 1989).
6   Although another section of the Right, notably GRECE in France, rather identifies with 'pagan Europe'.
7   Jack Lively, 'The Europe of the Enlightenment', *History of European Ideas* (Vol. I, no. 2, 1981), p. 93. 'Europe's distinction lay in its possession of truths which, while applicable to all humanity, were not presently available to all humanity', (p. 98).
8   T. Meyer, (ed.) *Fundamentalismus in der modernen Welt* (Frankfurt, 1989).

FRANCES WEBBER

From ethnocentrism to
Euro-racism

'We are moving from an ethnocentric racism to a Eurocentric
racism, from the different racisms of the different member states to
a common, market racism . . .'

A. Sivanandan[1]

In the aftermath of the Second World War, the various countries of
Europe looked to different sources of labour, depending on their
particular histories and economic relations with the rest of the world.
Britain and Holland looked to their colonies and ex-colonies, but in
the 1960s Holland took workers from southern Europe and North
Africa as well. Belgium and Switzerland looked to southern Europe,
to Spain, Portugal and Italy, all countries of emigration. Switzerland's
foreign population rose from 90,000 in 1950 to over one million (16 per
cent of its population) by 1973; in addition, there were nearly 200,000
seasonal workers in construction, agriculture, hotels and catering, and
100,000 frontier workers. France took labour from both sources – it
had three million foreign workers by 1970, one-third of whom were
non-European. West Germany took refugees from eastern Europe
until they were no longer enough, and then looked to the Mediterranean, with recruitment offices in Verona, Athens, Belgrade and
Istanbul. By the early 1960s, it was recruiting from North Africa as
well. Sweden, Finland, Denmark, Norway and Iceland set up the
Nordic Labour Market in 1954, providing free movement for work
within a common travel zone. The majority of migrant workers in

Frances Webber is a barrister and works closely with the London-based Refugee Forum.

Race & Class, 32(3), (1991)

Sweden were Finns, but workers came from Yugoslavia, Greece and Turkey too.[2] By the early 1970s, there were about eleven million migrant workers in Europe. In the words of *Fortune Magazine:* 'Migrant workers now appear indispensable to Europe's economy.'[3] One-seventh of all manual workers in Germany and the UK had come in as immigrants, and in France, Belgium and Switzerland, a quarter of the industrial workforce was immigrant.

Most industrialised European states controlled their migrant labour strictly under 'guestworker' systems, put in place shortly after the war. A government department, such as the French Office National d'Immigration (ONI) or the German Bundesaushalt fur Arbeit (BfA) recruited the workers on behalf of employers. Workers were accommodated in hostels by employers, were tied by their contracts to a specific job for a specific time and were required to leave the country at the end of the contract or if they were sacked. Germany revived its laws relating to slave labour, passed under the Third Reich in 1937. In theory, the ONI controlled all immigration for work in France, but, in practice, over 80 per cent of migrant workers there came as visitors, found jobs and regularised themselves – a simple and painless process while labour was still wanted. The same process happened in Belgium. Sweden did not have a guestworker system, relying on spontaneous immigration for its labour needs.

In Britain, controls on immigration were imposed sooner than in most other European countries. This was partly because the immigrants were settlers, not guestworkers. They had the rights of British subjects – to residence, to the franchise, to education for their children (who began arriving in the early 1960s), to social and welfare rights and housing (although these were often, in practice, denied). But it was also because they were black, not European: from the first, for Britain, immigration and race were synonymous. The Commonwealth Immigrants Act of 1962 for the first time limited the entry of (black) British subjects, and imposed on them the requirement of work vouchers. The system was tightened up throughout the 1960s and in 1971 immigration for work, 'primary' immigration, was all but abolished for black people.

In the rest of Europe, meanwhile,* an emerging two-tier workforce was slotted into place by the provisions of the EEC agreement of 1968, whereby citizens of member states were free to travel across the Community in search of work, while guestworkers remained hostage to the 'host' community. Nor, within that country, did they have any rights worth speaking of – although, by the early 1970s, they had been resident in these countries for many years, on renewed labour contracts, and had started sending for their families.

---

* Britain did not join the EEC till January 1973.

There were sizeable settled communities of Turks and North Africans, for instance, in the mining and manufacturing regions of Belgium, Holland, north Germany and in northern France – since large employers in the manufacturing industries wanted a trained and skilled workforce, not a high turn-over of unskilled, short-term workers. Governments and labour authorities, on the other hand, did not want foreigners to settle and bring their families, and favoured the rotation of temporary, unskilled and rightless workers. The result was that during these times of labour shortage, immigrant workers in some European countries gained limited rights of residence, though none had freedom of movement, and rights to family reunification were conditional on such things as adequate support and accommodation. Few countries had anti-discrimination legislation and those, like Britain, which did, gave it no teeth.

*   *   *

But even as workers had begun to settle, a fundamental shift was taking place in the nature of the economy and the type of workforce it required. If workers had been brought in to work in the factories and the mines, the heavy industries, in the 1950s and '60s, by the 1970s the imperatives of post-industrial society required that they be laid off or, preferably, laid back in their countries of origin. Belgium stopped immigration for work in 1974, and began deporting 'irregular' workers and prosecuting employers of those without work permits. Holland did the same. Sweden instituted restrictive policies for migrant workers in the mid-1970s; France tightened controls on the entry of immigrants from Africa in 1970 and 1972, and again in 1974. The only legal migration to Europe became that of family members, coming to join breadwinners who had gained settlement rights, and refugees.

It was a period that saw the rise of racist and fascist ideologies, and the equation, familiar to Britain, of black with crime and crime with illegal immigration, spread across Europe. It intensified in response to the arrival, from about 1980 onwards, of refugees from countries like Turkey, Sri Lanka and the Philippines; from Ghana, Zaire, Eritrea and Somalia in Africa, and from the Middle East. In December 1982, an editorial in the *Frankfurter Allgemeine* commented:

> the interchange between Slav, Romanic, Germanic and other Celtic peoples has become a habit. A tacit 'we-feeling' has arisen in one and the same European culture. But excluded from this are the Turk-peoples, the Palestinians, North Africans and others from totally alien cultures. They, and only they, are the 'foreigner problem' in the Federal Republic.[4]

Three years earlier, Margaret Thatcher had spoken of the

British people's fear of feeling 'rather swamped by people of a different culture'[5]. In 1981, her government removed British citizenship from people without an ancestral connection with Britain. France had introduced a voluntary repatriation scheme in 1977, and in 1980 the law was changed to allow French-born North Africans to be deported. In 1986, right-wing interior minister Charles Pasqua introduced a measure which removed basic rights of due process to immigrants facing deportation: one of the first deportations under the new law was a mass deportation of 101 Malians, chained together in a specially chartered aircraft. There were 17,000 deportations in the year after the Pasqua law came into force.

West Germany was the first to crack down on refugees. Its constitution guarantees asylum to political refugees; in addition, in common with all other western European countries, it is a signatory of the UN Convention on Refugees of 1951, and the Protocol of 1967. The Convention forbids the return (*'refoulement'*) of a refugee who is lawfully on the territory of a host state, to a country where he fears persecution. Under the Convention, a refugee is defined as someone who is outside his or her own country and is unable or unwilling to return, owing to a well-founded fear of persecution on grounds of race, religion, political beliefs or membership of a particular social group. Victims of civil war or natural disaster are not refugees under the Convention; nor is anyone a refugee until he or she has left his or her own country. Originally, the Treaty was limited to European refugees; the geographical limitation was removed by the 1967 Protocol, which all European states signed except Italy (which did not, therefore, recognise Third World refugees until it signed the Protocol in 1989). The Convention laid down no procedures for deciding if someone was a refugee or not. These omissions from the Convention – the lack of an obligation to admit refugees in the first place, the strict definition and the lack of procedures – have been exploited to the full as each European country in turn tries to deflect refugees from its territory on to someone else's.

In 1980, 100,000 asylum-seekers arrived in West Germany. In July of that year, West Germany imposed the first visa restrictions to prevent further arrivals, and began to make life as difficult and unpleasant as possible for asylum-seekers who had already entered. They had to wait for up to eight years for a decision on their application, during which period they could not work. Their social security allowances were less than the basic rate for Germans. In 1982, their freedom of movement was restricted; they were assigned 'common lodgings' in camps and were not allowed to leave without permission. The measures cut the numbers down to less than 20,000 by 1983. In addition, the number of successful applicants was down to less than 20 per cent. In August 1983, a Turkish asylum seeker,

Cemal Altun, killed himself after his application was rejected. (On appeal, he was posthumously granted asylum.)

In 1985, in response to a new 'influx' of asylum-seekers, mainly Tamils, through East Berlin, an agreement was reached whereby the East German authorities refused entry to transit passengers en route to West Germany, Denmark or Sweden unless they had visas for those countries. Then, in January 1987, fines were imposed on airlines carrying undocumented or inadequately documented passengers; Britain, Denmark and Belgium immediately followed suit. In October of that year, Lufthansa and Pan Am staff were moved to protest at the expulsion from Germany of an asylum-seeker 'bleeding heavily at the mouth and wrists, whose escorts forced him under a seat with their feet'. They claimed the right to refuse to take expelled asylum-seekers, saying they did not want to descend to 'the role of the train drivers transporting Jews to Auschwitz'.[6]

Where West Germany led, other states followed. In 1983-4 a French media campaign accused asylum-seekers of being scroungers and terrorists, and in its wake the percentage of asylum-seekers who were refused increased as the authorities demanded more and more documentary proof of persecution. A similar process went on in Britain, which in 1985 imposed visa restrictions on Tamils fleeing Sri Lanka (the first time visas were required from Commonwealth citizens). Denmark imposed visa requirements in 1986, created special 'camps' for refugees, and strengthened border controls to send away asylum-seekers coming in through Germany. Belgium's Zaventem airport, near Brussels, became notorious for its illegal return of asylum-seekers without allowing them to make their application, and a law of 1987, purporting to control the activities of the immigration police, in fact gave them wider powers to refuse entry and made their decisions less susceptible to judicial intervention. The Netherlands' Schipol airport (Amsterdam) gained an equally bad reputation for its detention and treatment of asylum-seekers, and the percentage accepted as refugees was down to under 20 per cent by the late 1980s, as criteria were applied more and more strictly.

In Europe as a whole, the percentage of asylum-seekers granted asylum has gone down from about 65 per cent in 1980 to around 10 per cent in 1990. West Germany now accepts only 3 per cent of those who apply. The late 1980s have also seen the growth of the RIO (refugees-in-orbit) phenomenon – asylum-seekers being shuttled from one European airport to the next and back again, as states argue about whose responsibility they are.

States on the southern geographic fringe of Europe – Spain, Portugal and Italy – which, in the earlier stages of European post-war reconstruction were sending countries, did not have an immigration 'problem' until recently. But, as their economies developed from

small-scale farming to the large-scale exporting of crops, intensive
tourism and modern industry, their need for labour has grown – a need
which could not be met internally, despite the migration from the
countryside to the city. In Italy, for example, the gap was filled mainly
by migrant workers from North Africa, who largely do the crop-
picking and processing of food for export. For, in the words of Italy's
interior minister, 'more and more Italians refuse humble and dirty
work'.[7] Precise figures are difficult to gauge – but some estimates put
Italy's immigrant workforce at around 1.2 million; Spain has around
three-quarters of a million.

Such workers, hitherto unregulated simply because they were so
necessary, have recently been rendered illegal. For, increasingly,
southern Europe is now seen by the rest of the Community as the
weak spot in Europe's defences, the bridge-head for an African
invasion of the continent, all the more serious given the moves to
abolish internal border controls. So, in 1989, a so-called amnesty for
illegal workers was announced in Italy, under which about 140,000
workers, mainly in the industrial north, have become regularised. But
employers in the agricultural south do not want regular, stable,
socially-protected workers and have, therefore, not cooperated. In
conjunction with the amnesty, tough new aliens' laws were announced, tying immigration more tightly to labour market needs
through a quota system. In February 1990, further measures provided
for the expulsion of illegal immigrants who had no means of support,
and in June, visas for North Africans and Turks were announced,
together with the establishment of computerised registration of
immigrants and the deportation of all those who had not regularised
themselves.

Spain, meanwhile, has recently spent 520m pesetas fortifying the
frontiers of its North African enclave, Melilla, with barbed wire,
closed-circuit TV and monitoring equipment, and has announced the
setting up of a marine guard to patrol all of the country's 240-plus
harbours. It has entered bilateral agreements with France to control
the illegal entry of Turks and Africans, and has established six
detention centres for those without papers and lacking means of
subsistence. The Spanish Committee for Aid to Refugees accused the
government in 1989 of carrying out 'an implacable and systematic
policy of expulsion of rejected asylum-seekers', and the Communist
Party said Spain was becoming 'the gendarme of Europe' in the face of
immigrants and political refugees from the Third World. In Portugal,
measures were announced in March 1990 to prevent the country being
used as a 'stepping stone' by immigrants from Africa and Asia to other
EC countries.

Evidently, the problem for an open Europe was 'how to close it –
against immigrants and refugees from the Third World'[8] – how to erect

a common policy, a common set of rules, a common administrative apparatus, informed by a 'common, market racism', to keep them out. To this end, heads of national police forces and intelligence services and representatives of national governments have been meeting to set up an intra-state apparatus outside the remit of the EC and, therefore, beyond its control. And it is to that aspect of the new Europe that the following article addresses itself.

References

Much of the information in this article has been drawn from *Migration Newssheet* and the resources of the Refugee Forum.
1   A. Sivanandan, 'The new racism', *New Statesman and Society* (4 November 1988).
2   Figures mostly from S. Castles, *Here for Good: Western Europe's new ethnic minorities* (London, 1984).
3   Quoted in J. Berger and J. Mohr, *A Seventh Man* (Harmondsworth, 1975).
4   Quoted in S. Castles, 'Racism and politics in West Germany', *Race and Class* (Vol. 25, no.3, 1984).
5   'World in Action', Granada Television (30 January 1978).
6   *CEDRI Bulletin* (August and December 1987).
7   Quoted in *Migration Newssheet* (5 October 1989).
8   A. Sivanandan, op. cit.
9   Ibid.

TONY BUNYAN

Towards an authoritarian European state

On 1 January 1993 the internal borders of the twelve countries in the European Community (EC) will officially come down allowing for the free movement of goods, services, capital and (some) people. The Treaty of Rome in 1957 marked the beginning of this process and the Single European Act of 1987 set out the fulfilment of economic union for a market of 330 million people with a potential to challenge and supplant the economic power of the USA and of Japan. On the one hand, there are the formal institutions of the EC – its Council of Ministers, Commission and Parliament – drawing their authority from the Treaty of Rome and embodying free market principles, quasi-democratic procedures and at least the promise of social liberalism. On the other hand, behind these formal institutions lurk the begin-nings of another state apparatus, made up of ad hoc and secretive bodies and separate inter-governmental arrangements, which reflects the repressive side of European political development and is largely unaccountable and undemocratic in its workings.

The main mechanisms of this 'other' Europe are the Trevi group of Ministers (1976), the Ad Hoc Group on Immigration (1986) and the Schengen Accord (1985 and 1990). Crucially, all focus on immigration in terms of a 'law and order' issue – alongside, in the case of Trevi and Schengen, terrorism, drugs, public order and the development of international cooperation on policing. The equation, familiar to Britain, of blacks with crime and drugs and terrorism, and all of that

Tony Bunyan is the Editor of *Statewatch* bulletin.

Race & Class, 32(3), (1991)

with illegal immigration,* has spread across Europe, so that it now forms a basis for the new European state.

The Trevi group

One of the earliest initiatives was the setting up in 1976, very much at the behest of the British government, of the Trevi group of interior ministers, with an original remit to serve as an inter-governmental forum to combat terrorism. Its name is not derived from the famous Roman fountain, but is an acronym for terrorism, radicalism, extremism and violence. As such, one of the first steps taken through Trevi was to establish a liaison network between the internal police and security agencies of the individual member states and a special secure communications system to link them. In Britain, this operates through the European Liaison section of the Metropolitan Police Special Branch under the direction of MI5.

By the time of the Single European Act in 1987, however, Trevi had expanded its remit from this initial focus on terrorism to embrace all the 'policing and security aspects of free movement', including immigration, visas, asylum-seekers and border controls. The logic behind this was that the principle of the free movement of people set out in the Act presumed that all those living and working inside the EC would be legitimate residents and not illegal immigrants or 'undesirables'. Otherwise, the removal of border controls between EC countries would raise the spectre not only of refugees from outside the EC seeking entry through the country with the most generous asylum policies, but also of what the House of Lords Select Committee on the European Communities called 'Euroscroungers', going from one European state to the next in search of better social benefits.[2] But since 'much of the problem with drugs and terrorism is home grown . . . a disease already grown inside the "soft centre"' of the EC, 'hardening the "shell" will do nothing to arrest the disease within' – and border controls will have to be 'internalised'.[3] Underlying these concerns there is an even more basic distrust among some member states, especially Britain, of the efficiency and political outlook of the police and security services in certain of their partner countries. One Scottish chief constable has spoken of the difficulty in explaining 'to a European mind our thinking at this end on what we regard as a threat'.[4]

As a result, what started off in 1976 as a means of constructing a hard 'outer shell' – to stop terrorists and other 'undesirables' from

---

* 'With so many immigrants in the EC, foreign terrorists can hide as easily as indigenous ones' (Major-General Clutterbuck).[1]

entering the EC from outside – has now become one for imposing internal controls as well, not least over the settled 'immigrant' communities of the different European countries.* This is reflected in the various working groups and other off-shoots that Trevi has spawned. Working Group 1 deals with terrorism and compiles in a common 'document' a joint analysis of threats 'both from within and outside the Community'. In addition, outside and in parallel with Trevi, there is now the Police Working Group on Terrorism, which is 'an alliance' of West European Special Branches, police agencies and security services. The information gathered and exchanged includes particulars of 'undesirable aliens from third countries'. Working Group 2 is concerned with police cooperation and the exchange of information, dealing with such matters as police equipment, computers, training, forensic science and public order (including public order weaponry and vehicles). Working Group 3, set up in 1985, deals with serious crime, including drug trafficking. Its work has led to EC drug liaison officers being posted to Third World countries and to the creation of national drugs intelligence units (a European unit is expected to follow). Working Group 4 (sometimes referred to as Trevi 1992) was established in April 1989 specifically to consider 'policing and security implications of the creation of the Single European Market' and to see how cooperation should be improved 'to compensate for the consequent losses to security and law enforcement' in the individual member states.

These groupings operate at different levels – ministerial; senior officials; and working parties made up of middle-ranking civil servants, police, and military, security and intelligence officers. A key contributing body from Britain is the Association of Chief Police Officers (ACPO) which, although it has no constitutional status, has been given a central role not only in the deliberations of Trevi (chief constables from ACPO's International Committee sit on all its working groups), but also in implementing consequent changes in British policing. The workings of Trevi are organised to parallel the six-monthly cycle of the European Commission and meetings of European interior and justice ministers, who can, therefore, formalise any decisions reached by its various groupings.

But, as recently explained to the Home Affairs Select Committee, 'Police matters are outside [European] Community competence and

---

* This dual purpose found formal expression through the European Commission in March 1985, when it spoke of the need to 'consolidate foreign communities which have acquired the characteristics of permanence' and to 'strengthen cooperation between member states in the campaign against illegal migration and clandestine employment'. However, the European Council of Ministers has shown a marked reluctance to work within the formal political machinery of the EC in developing such policies.[5]

so Trevi is independent of the European Community's institutional structure, and the EC Commission is not represented at any of its meetings.'[6] The ease with which the formal structures can be slipped in and out of has been described by one Home Office official as:

> the shuffling of chairs – if I can describe it – so that at a ministerial immigration meeting when the interior and justice ministers are present and the Commission is present, during the coffee break the chairs are shuffled and the Commission disappears and when they meet in their Trevi mode after coffee the Commission has gone.[7]

Indeed, the British government sees Trevi's 'distinctive strength' as lying in 'the informal, spontaneous and practical character of its discussions', especially as its deliberations are beyond both the scrutiny of the European Parliament and any questioning directed by member states' parliaments at individual ministers.[8] Or, as explained by Major-General Clutterbuck, Trevi 'succeeds in carrying out its work without media attention . . . and it provides machinery and authority for operations, especially police and intelligence services, to cooperate discreetly in their common professional aim of combating terrorism and crime'.[9] But a more critical view is offered by MEP John Tomlinson:

> They started off by justifying these private, secret discussions on the basis that they were dealing with questions of security . . . Then they extended it to discussions of drug policy . . . By the time they extended their agenda to a third subject, the coordination of immigration policy, then I regard the Trevi group as positively dangerous and undemocratic . . . they are managing to equate immigration policy and free movement of people with the same level of imperative secrecy as they are saying is necessary to have for counter-terrorist activities and counter drug activities . . .[10]

Trevi has also been the vehicle for agreeing various shared information systems, including a list of 59 countries whose nationals will require visas to enter the EC and a common list of 'undesirables' from non-EC countries (with each member state adding on its own list of additional 'undesirables' from within the EC). Other subjects covered by shared information are migratory flows, clandestine immigration networks and techniques used in the manufacture of travel documents. There will also be coordinated computer networks through which to administer these shared information systems. The new police national computer in Britain is already being planned to use the same software and equipment as other European security computers based in Wiesbaden in Germany (alongside Germany's own Bundeskriminalamt system).

The Ad Hoc Group on Immigration

In October 1986, again at the prompting of Britain, the interior ministers of the EC states re-formed themselves once again, into the 'Ad Hoc' or 'Working' Group on Immigration, this time with the aim of ending 'abuses of the asylum process'. In April 1987, the group agreed to sanctions on airlines bringing in undocumented asylum-seekers and to the coordination of the processing of asylum requests. In June 1990, this group produced the Convention Determining the State responsible for examining Applications for Asylum lodged in a Member State of the European Communities, which was duly signed in Dublin by all the EC countries. The convention, like the other agreements, is not within the competence of the EC institutions, notably the European Parliament. Under the convention, the first country to admit an asylum-seeker, in whatever capacity, becomes responsible for dealing with his or her application, regardless of any connections with other countries or personal wishes.

The body overseeing the work of Trevi and the Ad Hoc Group on Immigration, and other groups working on police and customs – the Group of Coordinators – was set up by the European Council in Rhodes in 1988. In its report to the European Council in Madrid in 1989, it set out a timetable of measures required by 1992 to protect the EC from immigrants and refugees. Measures it saw as essential included simplified or priority procedures for 'pre-screening' of asylum applications to weed out those considered 'clearly unfounded'; internal measures to offset illegal immigration and combat refugee and immigrant traffickers; and the determination of the member state responsible for removal of unwanted immigrants.

The Schengen agreement

Another mechanism of this emerging European state is the Schengen Accord, a separate inter-governmental agreement, first signed in 1985 between Germany, France, Belgium, the Netherlands and Luxembourg, to 'harmonise' policy on visas, coordinate crime prevention and search operations, in particular in connection with narcotics and laws governing their use, arms and explosives trade, and the registration of hotel guests. A supplementary agreement, Schengen II, was signed in 1990, containing legally binding 'counter measures' to close 'security loopholes' that will arise following the full abolition of border controls between the signatory states. What the supplement provides for is the exchange between member states of information on new asylum laws, on new arrivals and countries of origin of asylum-seekers, the emergence of significant groups of asylum-seekers, and information on individuals – identity, their application and its result. The Schengen countries have also agreed a common list of about 115 countries whose nationals will require visas to enter Schengen territory. They include most of the refugee-producing countries. In addition, a common list of 'undesirables', who will be refused entry to all Schengen states, is being drawn up.

The measures included in Schengen are significant, not least because the European Commission has acknowledged that they 'constitute a laboratory of what the Twelve [EC countries] will have to implement by the end of 1992, since the five [Schengen countries] are confronted with the same problems facing the Community'.*

Since 1985 the authorities of the Schengen countries have been meeting in working parties to agree common rules relating to a broad range of immigration, policing, security and judicial matters that will accompany the abolition of border controls between them. The Schengen rules determine who is to be allowed into the common travel area and for how long. Non-Schengen nationals will be admitted for three months if they have a visa and sufficient means to support themselves and to return home. If they are defined as undesirable by another member state, or as a suspected risk to public order, national security or relations with another member state, they are to be refused. 'Undesirable' is defined as someone from a non-member state who has been or who is likely to be refused entry to a member state. Transit passengers will only be admitted if they fulfil the conditions of entry to their destination and if their onward journey and their return to their own country are guaranteed, if they have sufficient means for their stay and for their return journey, and if they are not 'undesirable'. Carriers carrying passengers with false or inadequate documents will be fined. A three-month visa for a Schengen state is renewable only in exceptional circumstances, and freedom of movement across Schengen states for non-citizens is subject to compulsory registration with the authorities within three days of the person's arrival in his or her country of destination. Those who do not fulfil the conditions of stay in one Schengen country are to be removed from the whole Schengen area.

These rules will be enforced through mutual policing and security arrangements between the Schengen countries, backed by a powerful computerised intelligence and information system – the Schengen Information System – originally to be based at Wiesbaden, Germany, but now to be based at Strasbourg in France. The agreeement

* The Schengen network has recently been enlarged – Italy first expressed interest in joining in 1987 and was finally admitted in October 1990, after its implementation of tighter restrictions on immigrants and refugees. Spain, Portugal and Austria have also shown an interest in joining.

envisages the harmonisation of not only policies on visas and immigration but also the coordination of crime prevention and search operations – in particular, in connection with narcotics and laws governing their use, the arms and explosives trade and the registration of hotel guests. This may extend to include legal sanction for the police and other law enforcement agencies of one country to operate in another, including undercover work and the use of such means as observation across frontiers, infiltration of drug rings and Europe-wide police surveillance. Another clause deals with the need for mutual assistance between national intelligence agencies. Thilo Weichert, a German lawyer, comments that, '"Services" that are already out of control at a national level will be even harder to curb on a Europe-wide basis . . . It is likely that the focus of joint intelligence service operations will shift from counter-espionage to anti-extremist activity'.[11]

The computerised search apparatus of the Schengen Information System has been described as the 'most powerful instrument for turning the Community citizen without frontiers into an information subject'.[12] It will allow access in certain cases to unprotected data on an individual which may be based on 'intelligence' – that is, nothing more than suspicion. Yet the consequences for the individual could be arrest, extradition or refusal of entry in any of the participating countries. Recourse to the law will only be in the national courts, and then only in relation to the respective national authorities. The difficulties facing a person being held in one country, based on information passed on from another, in seeking legal remedies are clear. The scope of this information system – and the extent to which Schengen arrangements will encroach on internal affairs of each of the participating countries – is clear from a recap of the subjects and areas it will cover: aliens classed as 'undesirable'; asylum applications and refused applications; wanted criminals for prosecution, sentence, expelling or extradition; persons under surveillance; tracking of whereabouts (e.g., hotel registrations or the use of identity cards), and details of firearms and vehicles. In December 1989, the European Parliament passed a resolution* on the Schengen agreement which said that it could lead to discriminatory police actions, have a detrimental effect on the rights of refugees and migrant workers, and would endanger legal protection and the privacy of individuals.

---

* The resolution expressed concern: 'that the secret discussions, without democratic control by parliamentary supervision, on matters of police action, internal and external security and immigration, namely those affecting refugees, by member states acting outside the competence of the European institutions, within fora such as Schengen, Trevi and the ad hoc Immigration Group, violate the aforementioned conventions and democratic principles.'[13]

*   *   *

But even as the internal controls are being set in place for 1992, outside the remit of the EC, so also have the military and intelligence services of Europe begun priming themselves for new fields of operation. The Gulf crisis, in particular, has accelerated the process of creating a military role for the new Europe. EC member countries, operating through intergovernmental European political cooperation, are now seeking a common foreign and defence policy. As NATO has no powers to operate outside Europe and the Republic of Ireland is neutral, EC action in the Gulf has been coordinated through the Western European Union (WEU).*

Italy, which currently holds the EC presidency, is proposing a military role for the EC to tackle crises outside the Community. This has the backing of Sir Leon Brittan, vice-president of the Commission, who has called for the creation of a European Security Community to coordinate joint military policy and action and to replace the WEU:

> I see this as a forum to develop military integration in terms of joint forces and a specialisation of roles. It is time that the engine which has secured so much for Europe economically was harnessed so that its motive power can be felt in the area of security as well as foreign policy.[14]

The development of an EC military role would serve two functions, to act as the European arm of NATO and to provide a rapid deployment force outside of the EC. With the US's potential withdrawal from its role as global policeman to its specific spheres of influence (Central and South America and South-east Asia) will come the assumption of a new mantle by the EC countries in the fields of their old empires (Middle East, Africa and Asia). The weapons and technology of the cold war era will now be turned south on the countries of the Third World.

The EC's economic base, a common foreign policy and the development of the European defence 'pillar' of NATO – but with a remit to act worldwide – will allow Europe to deal with the US as an equal. Alongside this, the new European state is set to exclude Third World peoples from its shores and to create a system of internal controls which will criminalise black settlers and illegal immigrants alike.

---

* This was set up in 1955 and has nine EC member countries – excluding Ireland, Denmark and Greece. It was last activated during the Iran-Iraq war.

References

1 Richard Clutterbuck, *Terrorism, Drugs and Crime in Europe after 1992* (London, 1990), p.153.
2 House of Lords, Select Committee on the European Communities, '1992: border controls of people', HL Paper 90 (7 November 1989).
3 K.G. Robertson, *1992: the security implications* (London, Institute for European Defence and Strategic Studies, 1989), p.6.
4 House of Lords, op. cit., p.31.
5 European Commission, *Communication on guidelines for a community policy on immigration* (Brussels, March 1985).
6 House of Commons, Home Affairs Select Committee, *Practical police cooperation in the European Community*, Vol. II, 363-II (20 July 1990), p.5.
7 Ibid., p.90.
8 Ibid., p.5.
9 Clutterbuck, op. cit., p.7.
10 John Tomlinson, MEP, 19 September 1989.
11 Thilo Weichert, 'Europeanisation of the police: a possibility?' Paper for the Conference on the Policing of Europe, Strasbourg, 12-13 July 1990, p.10.
12 Ibid., p.10.
13 European Parliament resolution on the Schengen Agreement, December 1989.
14 *Independent* (14 September 1990).

The racist theme

NORA RÄTHZEL

Germany: one race, one nation?

The process of European integration is accompanied by two contradictory developments: the permeability of borders within the European community and the growing impermeability of the outer borders of this community (including the exclusion of the European population not considered to belong to Europe). These political perspectives, which tend to divide the European population into first- and second-class citizens and restrict migration from 'outside' Europe, call for political action on a European level. One condition for this is the knowledge of the differences and similarities in the respective European countries. In this context, my aim is merely to provide some basic information about the developments concerning migration into West Germany during the last twenty years and to situate them within the frame of general political events during that period.

The history of post-war migration

Nearly every account of migration to West Germany takes as its starting point the post-war contracts made between the West German state and a number of south European and north African countries to recruit workers for German industry.[1] But migration into West Germany actually started immediately after the Second World War with the arrival, between 1945 and 1949, of some nine million Germans, the majority of whom had been expelled from the then

* *Nora Räthzel* is at the Institut für Migrations-und Rassismusforschung, Hamburg, and is a member of the editorial group of *Das Argument*.

Race & Class, 32(3), (1990)

Polish territories as a reaction against the war and the occupation of the country by the fascist German state. Additionally, about three million East Germans, many of them skilled workers, fled to West Germany for political and/or economic reasons. But, following the building of the Berlin Wall in 1961, the number of people coming from East Germany fell from an average of 200,000 a year to about 20,000. This reduced level of migration was compensated partly by increased automation and partly by the entry of greater numbers of workers from southern Europe.[2] In the last two years, however, the situation has changed yet again, most spectacularly after the fall of the Berlin Wall in November 1989. Since 1987, almost 50 per cent of migrants have been either ethnic Germans from Eastern Europe (*Aussiedler*) or Germans from the GDR (*Übersiedler*).

The reason why these earlier large migrations are scarcely mentioned in the literature is because the migrants themselves were of German origin and were, therefore, not considered migrants. Migrants, on the other hand (and by the same token), were foreigners. Initially so-called 'guestsworkers', they were later identified as 'foreign workers' and then just as 'foreigners'. Furthermore, it is assumed that migration gives rise to 'problems', whereas the large number of post-war migrants were integrated in a fairly straightforward way. The 'social costs' of migration (of providing housing, for example) were dealt with – not discussed as insoluble, even though the country was much poorer then.

Thus, though there are around four million people living in West Germany as a result of immigration, it does not regard itself as a country of immigration. Consequently, what obtains in Germany is not immigration law but 'foreigners law' (*Ausländergesetz**), deriving ultimately from nazi legislation, more specifically from a regulation passed in the war legislation of September 1939 which related the presence of foreigners exclusively to the 'interests of the state', thus ensuring that they had no means of exercising any influence over their presence in Germany.[3] This principle is still in force, except for residents of the European Community (EC), who have the right of entry and of employment and self-employment. The law was recently modified (in April 1990), but it is worth discussing here, in some detail, the previous legislation since this was operative until so recently, and in any case illuminates much of the structure and the

* When the first contracts for workers were signed in 1955 and 1960, the *Ausländerpolizeiverordnung* (Foreigners Police Degree) of 1938 was still in force, allowing foreigners to live in the country as long as they showed themselves 'worthy of hospitality'. This vague formulation did at least enable foreign workers to exercise some influence on their residence in Germany by being 'worth it'. However, the autonomy this implied was not in the interests of the German state and of German capital, and the *Ausländergesetz* was introduced in 1965 to replace the legislation of 1938.

basic premises of the policy. According to the *Ausländergesetz*, those who wanted to enter the country needed to obtain a residence permit and, if they wished to work, a work permit before entry.

The procedures for obtaining residence and work permits were complex. There were different kinds of residence permits, limited, unlimited and, finally, the 'residence entitlement', which, with the exception of naturalisation, conferred on the foreign worker the highest degree of security. But even under this, 'foreigners' could be expelled if, for instance, they left the country for longer than six months, lost their passport, if it was not renewed, or if they committed a serious crime. (As from 1990, migrants with an unlimited residence permit have been given somewhat more security; but others are worse off.)

Only naturalisation can secure a foreigner's status as a resident, although there is no right to German citizenship. But people may apply for German citizenship if they have been living permanently in the FRG for at least ten years, are at least 18 years old, meet all sorts of conditions like knowledge of the German language, a reasonable flat, economic security, etc, and, in addition, have decided to orient themselves towards Germany and the German culture, have integrated themselves into German society and have a way of life which demonstrates no transgression of German law. The purpose of these restrictions is said to be the preservation of a homogeneous *Kulturnation*.[4]

These conditions and the high cost of naturalisation are some of the main reasons why only 2.9 per cent of the Italian, 2.8 per cent of the Spanish and 0.75 per cent of the Turkish population are naturalised.[5] The vast majority of foreigners now resident in West Germany are liable to expulsion. Although this has not been widely practised to date, it remains a constant threat.

During the recession of 1973, some Länder ruled by the Christian Democrats argued in favour of repatriating unemployed foreigners, but, in the end, this was not done for a number of reasons. First, if foreigners were to function as a reserve army of labour, it was preferable to retain those who were already accustomed to German life and work and who had achieved some skills, than to be forced to start the whole process of recruitment and training again. Second, there was fear of political opposition, not only from within the Federal Republic (FRG) itself but also from other countries, which would have been harsh in the light of German history. Third, the German government feared hostile reactions from countries of emigration, with which it needed to maintain good relations. But the legislation served to keep migrants in constant fear and uncertainty about their chances of staying in the FRG.

Since the recession of 1973, non-residents of the EEC have, in principle, not been allowed to enter the country to work. But there are a number of exceptions. These include (a) 'privileged foreigners', including citizens of countries with which the FRG has special agreements (eg, Switzerland, the US); 'homeless foreigners', made so by the Second World War; recognised refugees; stateless people, diplomats and members of foreign armed forces; (b) refugees seeking political asylum; (c) *Aussiedler* (ethnic Germans from Eastern Europe), and (d) *Übersiedler*, considered to be German citizens as citizenship of the GDR was never recognised.[6]

As the right of asylum for political refugees is written into the Federal Republic's constitution, a lot of fantasy had to go into restrictive legislation to reduce the number of asylum-seekers. Since 1980, the number of people who may be defined as political refugees has been gradually limited, with the result that, in 1987, 90.6 per cent of people seeking asylum were not granted political refugee status – a percentage which has even increased in 1990, to 96.5 per cent at the time of writing.[7]

Yet, despite the widespread withholding of formal refugee status, only a very small proportion of refugees are expelled. The others are granted permission to stay because they are political refugees according to the Geneva Convention (which the FRG has signed) and their expulsion could lead to prison or death. The logic of this practice is to discourage refugees from seeking entry into West Germany and to reduce the number of people who have the right to residence and work (rights granted only to those with recognised political refugee status).

Despite the continuing reduction in those granted refugee status, there is an on-going campaign to abolish this constitutional provision altogether, or to formulate it in a more restrictive way, on the grounds that it prevents asylum-seekers from being rejected, out of hand, at the border. In September 1990, the Social Democrat shadow chancellor proposed, for the first time in public, that the constitutional law should be changed. Countries in which there was no political persecution should be listed so that the authorities at border control could refuse entry directly to people coming from those countries. As I write, the initiative has not so far succeeded.[8] Other measures have included fining transport companies for bringing in people without visas from countries where these would normally be required – hardly something a refugee fleeing persecution is able to obtain before he or she leaves.

Refugees have also been discouraged from seeking to enter West Germany in a number of other ways. They are confined to camps and not allowed to travel more than a certain distance away from them and they are forbidden to work for five years (waiting for official refugee status can take that long, or even longer). In some states, like

Baden-Württemberg and Saarland, they receive only a very small state benefit in money, most of it being given in the form of food and clothes. In the words of Späth, former minister of internal affairs: 'The bush drums will say: Stay out of Baden-Württemberg. There you are put in a camp and given terrible things to eat, little money and no work permit.'[9] The German government has even distributed videos of the situation of refugees in German camps in Asian and African countries, in order to discourage people from coming to Germany.

Despite these restrictions, however, immigration overall has increased. In 1987, for example, a total number of 591,765 people entered West Germany. But, of these, 119,429 (20%) were Germans from all parts of the world and 158,352 (26.8%) were ethnic Germans from Eastern Europe; a further 105,771 (17.8%) were from EC countries and 65,507 (11%) came either from Africa or Asia; the remainder were from north and south America, Australia and New Zealand. Thus, in 1987, 46.8 per cent of immigrants were people with German passports or were defined as Germans. The number of asylum-seekers was 57,379 (9.6%).[10]

The point of going into numbers in some detail is not to play the 'numbers game' but to show that even the material basis for arguments about the 'floods' of Third World migrants pouring into Germany are false and biased.

When one looks at net migration, the same overall pattern holds true: around 52 per cent Germans or 'ethnic' Germans, nearly 10 per cent from the EC. The net figure amounts to only 32 per cent of the total number of inward migrants.[11] So that the argument that the 'boat is becoming too full', raised when figures for refugee migration are presented, is, on this showing, weakened still further. And, when one considers the size of the West German population as a whole, which has decreased from 62,101,400 in 1973[12] to 61,247,700 in 1987 (partly because of the decline in the birthrate, partly because the net balance of migration has been negative in nine years out of the fourteen), it becomes weaker still.

However, before dealing with the current tensions between economic and demographic reality, on the one hand, and nationalist sentiment, on the other, it is necessary to look back at the ways in which the issue of migration and settlement has been used on the German political scene over the past twenty years.

The political reaction to migration and settlement

One can distinguish a number of different stages in the West German state's handling of, and reaction to, migration.[13] The first, from 1945 to 1962, saw the migration of Germans from Eastern Europe and the GDR, which apparently caused only minor problems and was not the subject of major political debate. The second, from 1955 to 1973, was one in which workers were recruited mainly from southern European countries, and were meant to stay only temporarily. They were housed in special camps and were not supposed to bring in their families, thus imposing no 'social costs' on German society. This original system of 'rotating' foreign workers worked partly, but to what extent it is difficult to determine.[14] Employers, by and large, found it easier and cheaper to keep on an already-trained workforce, instead of recruiting afresh every five years; moreover, migrants began to settle and bring their families in.

Nevertheless, the notion of temporary recruitment survived, partly because, during the first economic crisis after the Second World War (in 1967/68), large numbers of migrant workers did leave the country. But during the second economic crisis of 1972/73 (after the rise in oil prices), workers did not leave. On the contrary, when recruitment was halted in 1973, Turkish workers who had previously hesitated to bring their families in then did so, afraid that this might not be possible in the future and that, if they left the FRG, they might not be able to return.

The fact that the 'guestworkers' settled down, that for various reasons it was not feasible to send them back, meant that the perception of migrants and their role in German society had also to be modified.

In 1978, a commission was set up under the leadership of the former ministerpräsident from Nordrheinwestfalen, Kühn, who in 1979 produced the famous Kühn-Memorandum. After thirty-four years of migration (twenty-four of which had also seen the migration of non-German peoples into the FRG), this document acknowledged officially for the first time that there had been immigration into West Germany. On this basis it called for:
– more attempts to integrate migrants, especially children and young people;
– legislation giving migrants some security over residence;
– the right to German citizenship for immigrants' children born in the FRG;
– the right to participate in local elections after a longer period of residence.

But the government (a coalition of the Social Democrats and the Liberal Party) rejected the proposals of its commission; instead, it reinforced further the old principles of its so-called foreigners' policy: (1) to prevent further migration, (2) to encourage voluntary repatriation, (3) to better the economic and social integration of those who had lived in the FRG for many years and (4) to make the right of residence more precise.

The principles of the new 'foreigner policy' were published in

February 1982 amidst fierce campaigning against the presence of migrants, especially refugees. This had begun in 1980 after the Social Democrats had suffered severe election losses – though they were still able to form a coalition government with the Liberal Party. Fears of '*Überfremdung*' (aliens taking over) were whipped up by conservatives at a time when the ruling Social Democrats were in retreat. The latter, who had been in power since 1969, were faced with the erosion of their traditional working-class support as the nature of employment and the labour force changed and the numbers of employed workers declined. At the same time, they lost the support of the more intellectual, left liberal strata over, for example, the introduction of increasingly repressive legislation (*Berufsverbote*, anti-terrorist laws) which, while losing them their erstwhile left-wing support, was not deemed sufficiently severe to win over the conservatives. In the 1980s, support was further diminished as a result of military policy – the acceptance of the Nato decision to station new missiles in West Germany. Finally, the Social Democrats' educational reforms – one of the party's main planks – came under attack as unemployment in general and among academics increased. Attempts to improve the education of working-class children were questioned not only by wealthy parents but by progressive teachers, who saw it as transforming schooling into a uniform, technical, mass process. And, while the Green Party (founded in 1979) sought to win over those who wanted a more radical alternative to the Social Democrats, far greater numbers turned towards the politics of privatisation and individualisation offered by the conservatives.

In this situation – of the breaking up of old, and the forming of new, political loyalties – the political discourse over asylum-seekers was the focus around which both the Social and the Christian Democrats tried to form new political bases for themselves.

For the conservatives, migrants were defined as *asylanten*, asylum-seekers who were not really political refugees but just trying to live off the wealth of 'our' country. The FRG was, it was argued, too small and not rich enough to accept more people coming in. Refugees were criminalised, seen as drug dealers – or 'drug containers' as the Senator for Internal Affairs in West Berlin, Lummer, later termed them.[15] The Left (Social Democrats, mainly) criticised such arguments, but it also used the presence of migrants to construct its version of political reality, aimed at gaining the support of left-liberal voters. It argued that too many immigrants engendered *Ausländerfeindlichkeit* (hostility to foreigners), forcing politicians to become more conservative and enabling the Right to gain hegemony by exploiting the fears of the population. Southern European migrants, besides, were not so used to democratic traditions and would tend to weaken further these already weak institutions. Images of migrants were used to define, by contrast, the Left's own political democratic position: migrants were the 'mirror', that showed the opposite of what a good German democrat was fighting for. The consensus of all parties – except the Greens – was that the country could endure no more *Ausländer*.

This is not to say that there was a conspiracy between the 'Left' and the 'Right'* over defining the presence of migrants as problematic. But what resulted was a kind of unintended 'cooperation' in constructing a negative image of the migrant. Thus, the liberal and highly respected newspaper *Die Zeit* published an article by the general secretary of the German Red Cross arguing that 'non-Central European people' should be repatriated to avoid a break in German history.[16] About the same time, the Heidelberger Manifesto was published. The work of a number of professors from different universities, it argued that the 'mixture' of different cultures would be damaging to everybody: all people should live in their 'own' place. And whereas the public version of their manifesto talked about different cultures, their private version (leaked to the press) discussed peoples as biological and cybernetic systems with different traits passed on to subsequent generations through genes and through tradition.[17] The NPD attempted to collect signatures for a referendum, *Volksbegehren Ausländerstop*, on the subject. And the Social Democratic head of the Hessen government stated: 'As long as I have something to say, no Turk will enter this country any more.'[18]

In opinion polls, more than 62 per cent agreed that there were too many foreigners in the country and more than 50 per cent said that they should be sent back; the same percentage believed that the Christian Democrats would be more likely to achieve this.

Accordingly, the 'foreigner problem' was one of the main issues that the Christian Democrats promised to deal with. When Chancellor Kohl took power in Autumn 1982 (the Liberal Party had broken its coalition with the Social Democrats in order to form a new one with the Christian Democrats), he declared: 'The number of our foreign compatriots [sic] must be diminished.'

After this coalition had won the elections in 1983, a new commission was set up to find out (a) how integration could be improved; (b) how willingness to return could be strengthened, and (c) how the number of foreigners could be reduced. Apart from the constant whittling away of the right to asylum, the only measure to be taken was the *Rückkehrprämie* (premium for return), under which all unemployed foreign workers would be given DM10,500 (£3,500) and DM1,500 for each child to leave Germany. But they had to leave the country as soon as possible – if they remained for more than two

---

* Using these categories in Germany is somewhat problematic as their meaning in practical politics is constantly shifting.

months after becoming unemployed, this amount reduced by DM1,500 each month.[19] Workers from Portugal and Turkey could get back money they had paid into pension schemes, but not the employer's contribution; and they had to give up future rights to an old age pension. All in all, it was not a tempting bargain and not as many left as envisaged. One year later, the scheme was abandoned.

One major reason why the numbers of migrants could not be reduced was that, despite unemployment rates which particularly affect migrant workers (many of whose jobs are disappearing with automation and the decline in heavy industry), they are still badly needed. As the total population declines, expanding sections of industry, such as electronics, fear labour shortages over the next decades. Hence, senior journalist Roland Tichy of the business weekly, *Wirtschaftswoche*, could argue in his book, *Ausländerrein* (Let foreigners in), that the decline in population in Europe, coupled with its expanding production, calls for further recruitment of workers from other countries, including the so-called Third World.

Nor was the Christian Democrat Party able at first radically to alter the legislation on foreign workers, despite imaginative drafts provided by the ministry of home affairs – in one of which, children more than 6 years old would be refused entry to join their parents. For the Liberal Party, the Christian Democrat's coalition partner and erstwhile partner of the Social Democrats, refused to support such measures. It chose this issue on which to display its liberal credentials and distinguish itself from the CD, in order to regain credibility among its supporters. It had been seen as having betrayed its liberal principles when it reneged on its coalition with the Social Democrats, and lost much of its traditional support.

Aussiedler und Übersiedler

The rapid collapse of the Communist regimes of Eastern Europe and the consequent opening up of their borders, and the dramatic developments in East Germany, culminating in the tearing down of the Berlin Wall, have added another whole dimension to the complexities surrounding the migration issue. The political consensus characterising all foreign workers and asylum-seekers as a threat to German prosperity and a drain on German resources has had to be redefined (while keeping the ideology underlying it in place).

For this consensus has been put under pressure not only by economic realities (the continuing need for cheap labour to offset demographic decline in a climate of rising material expectations), but also by the political necessity of welcoming, first the ethnic Germans from the former Communist regimes and, second, of giving full rights to Germans from East Germany. The FRG never officially recognised the German Democratic Republic (GDR) as a separate state and always called for full rights for East Germans to enter West Germany.

This rapid influx of ethnic Germans and East Germans may have met the needs for labour (and, in the process, rendered the situation of Third World workers and asylum-seekers even more marginal), but it has posed further problems of explanation for the politicians – who, whilst proving conclusively that the country could no longer accommodate foreign workers and refugees, had also to argue that a large migration of ethnic Germans, *Volksdeutsche*, posed no problem. Suddenly, there was money to fund housing programmes and provide teachers for German-learning programmes (as the *Aussiedler*, the ethnic Germans, often did not speak the language): as much as DM100m in 1988 and DM202m in 1989.

To square the circle, the government started a mass advertising campaign. For people had been told for years that too many migrants were entering, that borders have to be closed, etc. Now, suddenly, they were told that 'we' had a lot of space, and money, to 'host' our 'brothers and sisters' whom 'we' had always wanted to come; that it was a shame that such a rich country could not give houses and jobs to German compatriots. After all, (1) the *Aussiedler* were Germans not foreigners, to receive them was an act of patriotism not just humanity; (2) they were young and had exactly the qualifications that were needed, and (3) the German population was decreasing, so that increasing numbers of pensioners would have to be supported economically by a shrinking workforce. The *Volksdeutsche* from Eastern Europe were the answer: they would solve all the demographic problems of West Germany. Figures were circulated to show that one million *Aussiedler* would be just enough to balance out the pension schemes.

While discussion was still going on about the integration of the ethnic Germans into West German society, the Hungarian government opened its borders to the GDR in August 1989. For the next four months, the first report in the daily news bulletin was the number of East Germans who had crossed over the day before. At the beginning, they were greeted with joy, as 'brothers and sisters' finally coming to live in freedom. But this attitude changed after the fall of the Wall in November 1989. In October 1989, according to opinion polls, 63 per cent of West Germans agreed East Germans should be accepted; by February 1990, this had dropped to 22 per cent, and even among those who felt their own economic situation was 'very good' or 'good', 70 per cent claimed that *Übersiedler* got too much in the way of state hand-outs.[20]

Once unification came on to the agenda, the political interest that had seen migration from the GDR as destabilising of the Communist system and, therefore, to be encouraged went into reverse. Now, in the face of growing resentment against *Übersiedler* in the West German population, politicians encouraged East Germans to stay at home. For one thing, if capital investment was going to be made by West German capital into East Germany and Eastern Europe, it made sense to keep the qualified workforce there, rather than allowing it to migrate, willy nilly, into West Germany.

Hence, in February 1990, several measures were taken to make moving from the East to the West less attractive. For instance, unemployment money and sickness benefit, to which East Germans had had the same right as West Germans as soon as they settled in the FRG, was replaced by 'integration money' – a lump sum of DM1,000-1,200. The same pattern occurred with ethnic Germans. Here, as well, restrictions were imposed, first by the Länder governed by the Social Democrats. But what is interesting about these restrictions is the basis on which they were imposed; the concept of 'Germanness' and the German nation which underlies them.

What is specific about the concept of the German nation – as compared, for instance, to France – lies in the fact that it is constructed biologically. German nationals are defined by their origin: one can only be born a German; whereas the French idea of nation is constructed politically, which means that anybody ready to accept French culture and assimilate to it can become a French citizen. So that while the children of migrants born in France have a right to opt for French citizenship, naturalisation is difficult to impossible under German legislation.[21]

But the issue is more complicated than that. The idea of the German *'Volk'* as the only true Volk in Europe, defined by a common origin and a common destiny of teaching democracy to the rest of the world, has been formulated by many writers and thinkers. Yet a German nation state composed of this original German Volk never existed. There were, in fact, a number of different nation states where German-speaking citizens were the majority (language was one of the main elements that defined Germanness). There were also, within those nation states, minorities of non-German origin who, nonetheless, had German citizenship as well as special minority rights. In the constitution of the Weimar Republic, they were addressed as the non-German part of the Volk who were guaranteed the right to develop their own culture and their own languages in the schools and institutions of the state. Thus, there was a contradiction between the philosophy of the German nation as a nation of people with a common origin, and the reality, which was that of several nations consisting of ethnic and non-ethnic German citizens. The German Volk consisted of Germans and non-Germans together.

It was not till 1934 and 1935 that German citizenship was restricted to those of German blood, which excluded Jews and Gypsies whose citizenship was thus abolished. What is presented as the time-honoured tradition of German citizenship defined by German birth is simply a product of German fascism, as least as far as the legislation is concerned.

Indeed, citizenship of Germany as a national entity is, in reality, the achievement of fascist legislation. Before 1934, the citizenship of the Länder which made up the German Reich had priority. One became a citizen of a Land (Hessen, Hamburg, etc) by birth or by jus soli and only on this basis, a member of the German Reich. One of the first acts of the Nazi regime was to abolish the citizenship of the Länder and institutionalise the wider German citizenship – at the same time, defining it as only for those of German blood. Today, the ethnic Germans have to prove their Germanity and right to citizenship by presenting papers – which derive directly from the fascist period – in which they are defined as Germans. After the occupation of Poland, the population was registered according to their 'German blood' on different lists (Volksliste 1/4). Volksliste 3 included those who had 'some German blood' but had proved faithful to Germany and could hope to be naturalised. Now, in the current phase of restricting ethnic German migrants, people registered on this list (that is about half of those coming from Poland) are no longer recognised as Germans in Länder governed by the Social Democrats, such as Hamburg, Bremen and Saarland. Thus, the wheel has come full circle, only now it is the Social Democrats who reproduce the purely biological construction of German citizenship that was first enacted by the 'Nürnberger Reichs-gesetze' in 1934.

Reunification and racism

The discussions about different groups of German migrants, and especially about how German reunification should proceed, have, at one level, taken the focus of debate away from the so-called *Ausländer*, but, at another, fuelled an increasingly virulent racism against them.

After seven years of Christian Democrat/Liberal Party government, where one right-wing proposal after another to amend the *Ausländergesetz* had been rejected by pressure groups from the church, social service organisations and the trades unions, as well as the ombudsman for 'foreigners', new legislation regulating their status was agreed between the coalition partners; it was allowed only three months to pass through parliament. Public opposition to it was weak, coming mainly from those concerned with the social welfare of foreigners and immigrant organisations. Demonstrations were also supported superficially by the Social Democrats and the trades unions, neither of whom, however, attempted to use their constitutional or industrial power to effect any real changes. The unions threatened: 'If [certain] paragraphs are not altered, we might not be able to consent to the legislation.' Hardly a statement to set the Rhine on fire.

On 26 April 1990, the new *Ausländergesetz* was passed in Parliament. There is no space here to go into it in detail, but, in principle, the law provides a differentiated instrument for the regulation of migration as well as for the residential status of migrants.

Those who are neither in possession of a West German passport nor defined as Germans now needed a visa to enter the FRG, except for nationals of the EEC or states with which the FRG had special agreements (West European countries, Australia, New Zealand, Israel, Japan, Canada and the US).[22] There are a number of reasons why a residence permit may be refused: most importantly, if migrants cannot prove that they can maintain themselves by employment, with their own money, or through the support of a friend or family member. In this context, the conditions under which work permits are issued are crucial. But these are left entirely at the discretion of the minister for internal affairs who can, according to the interests of the state, restrict permits to certain occupations, and to certain groups of foreigners. He can determine the character and duration of the residence permit and exclude or limit the issuing of an unlimited residence permit. In other words, foreign workers, except for a very small minority, can be treated even more absolutely as disposable units of labour; they can be repatriated or 'rotated' at will – a demand hitherto voiced in public only by the extremist right-wing Republican Party.

Although the law was meant ostensibly to give greater security of residence to those who had been living in the country for a long time or had been born there, it only did so to a very limited extent. Migrants who already have a relatively secure, unlimited residence permit have been given more security and it is easier for them to apply for German citizenship (though they still have no right to it). But for those not in this category, the connection between a residence permit and '*ausreichendem Wohnraum*' (sufficient space to live in) can prove a major obstacle. As of now, every 'foreigner' aged from 6 months to 16 years also needs a residence permit. Thus, a family whose flat was judged sufficient may, after the birth of a baby, be liable for expulsion – on the grounds of inadequate living space.

The situation of migrant workers in East Germany, brought in on contract and as students (mainly from Vietnam, Cuba, Mozambique, North Korea and Poland) and constituting about 1 per cent of the East German population, was in legal terms even worse. They were not allowed to make any contact with the German population and had to live isolated in special hostels. Now, with the collapse of the old regime, which defined itself as anti-racist and anti-fascist, but attempted to implement this policy by force and diktat, has come a resurgence of neo-fascism and racism. And, whereas in the past the government might at least, by pretending to international solidarity, have sheltered Third World migrants from direct physical abuse and attack, now they are increasingly vulnerable. Free, in theory, to walk the streets, live anywhere, visit restaurants, etc, in practice, they once again dare not leave the security of their hostels at night, even in numbers. And, of course, in all the pecking order of 'Germanity', they come nowhere.

Meanwhile, migration into East Germany from other Eastern European countries, far more drastically impoverished than it, has increased dramatically. In May, it was estimated that about 700 people were entering the country ever week.[23]

As East Germany has to adjust its legislation to that of West Germany (the territory of the GDR has already been written into the Schengen Treaty of June 1990),[24] one can foresee that economic and political interests will come into conflict. Whilst the first tend to be in favour of migration in allowing enterprises maximum choice over their workforce, political interests will tend to restrict migration, fearing the destabilisation of social peace – a fear that has to be seen in the context of growing racism in both East and West Germany. The East German 'brothers and sisters', it is argued in West Germany, can do the jobs that were formerly done by foreign immigrants.

The reconstruction of Germanness

What we are witnessing today is, in part, the reconstruction of what it means to be German. This new and changing situation is creating new definitions of who 'belongs' and who does not. I have already argued that the definition of German citizenship as such dates from fascism. Allegiance was initially to one's Land; only with fascism did the German Reich become paramount. Yet implicit in nearly all the literature is that there is a tradition of German citizenship dating back some 100 years to Germany's initial formation. The concrete history, of fascist political and administrative manipulation on which this exclusive citizenship was forged, is left out, while its product, the creation of a homogeneous nation-state, defined by biological origin, is seen to be the most self-evident and hallowed tradition. How has this come about?

It is, perhaps, related to the concept of the FRG as the follower of the pre-fascist German Reich. The year of the Federal Republic's founding was seen as the new beginning when all the past was overcome – when man, in fact, was reborn without sin. The official, dominant ideology is that there are no traces of fascism in Germany

any more and, therefore, also no racism, as anti-Semitism, the form racism took during fascism, is overcome. For, implicit in the idea of racism is a social practice and structure which can be related to such practices and structures in the past. And that past is over, done away with. What German intellectuals do acknowledge, however, is the existence of *Ausländerfeindlichkeit* – hostility to foreigners.*

What has this to do with the current debate raging round issues of who is German? Simply this, that, first, no connections can be made between what is happening with the rise of racism today and the past; all meaningful continuities and connections have been deliberately blanked out. Second, the politics of defining the German nation by legislation, as from a blank sheet, and excluding those not so defined, have been so successful as to become the unquestioned commonsense of the vast majority of West Germans. Third, this national self-definition, this national idea of Germany, has completely obliterated the reality of Germany as a country of immigration. Thus, while the Federal Republic claims not to be a country of immigration, no less than 15 per cent of its workforce are migrants. Consequently, concern focuses mainly on 'integrating' migrants to keep in place the homogeneity of the *Kulturnation*, while racism itself is untackled; indeed, racism does not exist, only *Ausländerfeindlichkeit*. It is within this logic, of the German nation as having a homogeneous population of German citizens, that battles are fought between those wanting to preserve such homogeneity, and those on the Left who challenge this notion by rejecting any notion of national identity at all, because they see it as so closely bound up with the form of the state.

This broad consensus that there is a homogeneous German state, the failure to recognise West Germany as a country of immigration like any other European state, the refusal to acknowledge that it has a non-German population that will not go back must be seen as the background for more recent political developments.

On the level of popular consciousness, it was quite common to define Germanness as referring to inhabitants of the German republic, holding a passport delivered by the West German authorities. Although people knew that there were other Germans living on the other side of the Iron Curtain, this was not a great factor in everyday life or in the definition of Germanness. The notion of 'us', for West Germans, was connected with *Wirtschaftswunder*, a stable DM, economic growth, etc. This image held true in other countries as well, even in Eastern Europe where, complained citizens of the GDR, they were not regarded as real Germans since they did not have real DM.

Within this rather restricted notion of Germanness, where biological and cultural homogeneity was connected overwhelmingly with

---

* See Notes and documents section.

the West German state and economic system, it was also quite clear
who did not belong, who was to be considered as the 'Other' –
everybody who did not have a birthright to a West German passport,
no matter how long they had been living and working in the country,
no matter whether they had been born there. There existed a
racialised picture of this Other, dark-haired, from the poor South,
underdeveloped, not speaking the language properly, doing the dirty
jobs, of the Muslim religion. In short, the Other was Turkish, and all
other migrants could be constructed as more or less Turkish, that is
more or less under-developed, more or less assimilated.

Under the pressure of recent events, these old assumptions are now
breaking up. The arrival of ethnic Germans in large numbers first
contradicted the stereotype that all Germans were German-speaking
people, socialised by a western capitalist lifestyle. Thus, if the
presence of *Aussiedler* was to be legitimised politically, either the
notion of Germanness had to be broadened, or, as Lafontaine
(shadow chancellor of the Social Democrats) demonstrated, they had
to be excluded from belonging to the nation. Moves aimed at
exclusion proved to be popular, as elections in the Saarland showed,
for they responded to the fears among the indigenous German
population of losing some of their economic wealth through the
migration of the ethnic Germans. In this context, the migration of the
East Germans at first seemed to offer a solution: now a distinction
could be made between the ethnic Germans and 'real Germans' who
spoke the language and came from a country that, in spite of political
differences, had always claimed itself as German. Indeed, the East
Germans were initially spoken of as more German than the West
Germans; they had preserved the old German virtue of industrious-
ness and had not been corrupted by the good life of the consumer
society.

At the time of writing, the great majority of West Germans
welcome unification, but that same majority object to further immigration from the country they are to be united with. In the course of
extended immigration, East Germans seem to have lost their Germanness and become the Other. Now they are not seen as embodying the
typical characteristics of the true industrious German, but as possess-
ing a number of negative attributes. They do not know how to work
properly, they find the pace of an efficient work process intolerable,
they put their personal interests above the interests of the enterprise,
they do not identify with their work. Employers are quoted as saying
that they are never going to employ anybody from East Germany
again. Suddenly, East German qualifications are not just what is
needed but are old-fashioned, useless for hi-tech production processes.[2]

All these negative characteristics, however, have to do not with their being 'German by blood', but with their being socialised by the Communist system. East Germans are considered as socially and culturally different, not different by nature. The result is that the concept of Germanness becomes yet further diffused. The biological and social construct of 'the German' are no longer identical. Whereas, in the past, the West German was 'the German' per se, now there are three different images competing: the modern successful West German, the hidebound, out-of-date East German, and the not-really-German-at-all ethnic German. In both East and West Germany, nationalism has come to be associated mainly with economic interests. Whilst Social Democrats in West Germany have won elections by playing down any broader considerations and stressing what nationalism will cost economically, Christian Democrats in East Germany have won elections by promoting nationalism as a means of increasing wealth. One nation – yes, but for West Germans, without paying and without having to bear the presence of the other German.

References

1   See U. Mehrländer, 'Auslanderpolitik und ihre sozialen Folgen' in H. Griese, *Der Gläserne Fremde* (Leverkusen, 1984), p.89ff; but see also U. Herbert, *Geschichte der Ausländerbeschäftigung in Deutschland (1880-1980)* (Berlin/Bonn, 1986).
2   See Herbert, ibid.
3   F. Franz, 'Ausländerrecht. Kritische Bilanz und Versucheiner Neuorientierung', in Griese, op. cit., p.73ff.
4   R. Banck, *Zur rechtlichen Lage ausländischer Arbeitnehmer* (München, 1987).
5   H. Kreutz, 'Europäische Integration, Weltoffenheit und nationale Indentität. Wie deutsch ist die Bundesrepublik? Wie deutsch ist die Bundesrepublik? Wie deutsch soll sie sein?', in P. Bocklet, *Zu Viele Fremde im Land* (Düsseldorf, 1990).
6   R. Banck, op. cit.
7   *Frankfurter Allgemeine Zeitung* (13 October 1990).
8   See *Tageszeitung* (25 August 1990) and *Frankfurter Allgemeine Zeitung* (13 October 1990).
9   See W. Baumgarten, J. Körner and G. Weiler, *Ein Jahn Abschreckungslager Thiepal-Kaserne Tübingen* (Tübingen, 1982), p. 64.
10   Calculations based on Statistisches Bundesamt, 'Bevölkerung und Erwerbstätigkeit. Fachserie 1, Reihe 1' (Gebiet und Bevölkerung, 1987), pp. 153-200. See also 'Bundesamt für die en Annerkennung ausländischer Flüchtlinge' in M. Schöttes and A. Schulze, 'Asypolitik in Daten und Fakten', *Eine Zusammenfassung statistischen Materials* (Berlin, Institut für Vergleichende Sozial forschung, undated).
11   Statistisches Bundesamt, op. cit., pp. 181-6.
12   Ibid, p. 200.
13   See also Mehrlander, op. cit., S. Castles, *Migration und Rassismus in Westeuropa* (Berlin, 1987).
14   Kreutz (op. cit., pp. 32-3) states that between 1960 and 1986 15m non-German persons entered the FRG, but the number of non-German residents was only 4m in 1986, meaning that more than 75% of those who entered the country left it again. As these calculations do not distinguish between people coming in as, e.g., asylum-seekers or contract workers, they do not tell us to what extent the

'rotation principle' was effective concerning workers.

15 *Der Spiegel* (No. 35, 1986).
16 H. Leuninger, 'Medien und Ausländer – eine Kritische (Nach) Lese', in Griese, op. cit.
17 A. Kalpaka and N. Räthzel, 'Wirkungsweisen von Rassimus und Ethnozentrismus', in Kalpaka and Räthzel (eds.), *Die Schwierigkeit, nicht rassistisch zu sein* (Leer, 1990). See also R. Miles and N. Räthzel, 'Migration and the articulation of racism' in S. Bolaria (ed.), *World capitalism and the international division of labour* (Toronto, 1990).
18 D. Thränhardt, 'Ausländer als Objekte deutscher Interessen und Ideologien', in Griese, op. cit.
19 S. Castles, op. cit.
20 *Der Spiegel* (26 February 1990).
21 R. Brubaker, *Immigration and the Politics of Citizenship in Europe and North America* (University Press of America, 1989); Banck, op. cit.
22 Banck, op. cit., p. 5.
23 *Frankfurter Allgemeine Zeitung,* (18, 19 May 1990).
24 *Frankfurter Allgemeine Zeitung* (21 June 1990).
25 *Der Spiegel 8/44* (19 February 1990).

CATHIE LLOYD and HAZEL WATERS

France: one culture, one people?

Racism and immigration have been crucial issues in French politics throughout the 1980s. But with the rise of the right-wing Front National (FN) following its by-election victory at Dreux in September 1983, there has been a legitimation of racism and violence which has reached alarming proportions. At the same time, laws passed in 1981 by the Mitterrand government have enabled people under attack to organise themselves more effectively (the 1939 law prohibiting people who were not French nationals from forming associations was repealed) and political participation of immigrants or people of immigrant origin is now on the political agenda.

At the centre of recent debate has been the position of people of Muslim origin in the secular state schools, particularly over girls' right to wear religious headscarves (*hijab*) on school premises. Muslim girls who wear the headscarf have been sent home from school. This 'threat' to French values has unleashed a new wave of support for the FN and fomented the debate about the 'integration' of 'immigrant' populations in France, which largely ignores the fact that a large community of different origins has been born and brought up in France and poses the question: what do the French mean by integration?

The debate about integration highlights one of the central problems in analysing racism in France: an intolerance of other cultures is

Cathie Lloyd is a member of the Campaign Against Racism and Fascism who is currently researching on the French Left and immigration. *Hazel Waters* is Deputy Editor of *Race and Class*.

Race & Class, 32(3), 1991

expressed in the name of the progressive and rationalist values associated with the 1789 Revolution. So, for those whose cultural frame of reference was formed by the Enlightenment, other cultures with a different reference point were inevitably seen as backward and lower down the scale of human progress – to be assimilated as rapidly as possible to the values of the Enlightenment, which were held to be universal, transcending nationalist sentiments and, therefore, of general application. Thus, wearing the headscarf in school was seen as a religious observance, inimical to the concept of a secular state education, which had been established on the separation of Church and State in 1905.

This progressive principle was part of a settlement between religious (Catholic, Christian) and secular authority and took little account of any other denomination or religious grouping. But today, with about two million Muslims living in France, about half of whom have French nationality,[1] this settlement has now reached a crisis of legitimacy. Even those who argued for a 'new secularism', based on a pluralist approach, did so by stressing that Muslim girls would never get the opportunity to learn the values of the French Enlightenment if they were forced into Muslim schools. According to Harlem Désir, 'It's in the framework of state education . . . in confrontation with another universe from that of the family, through the spirit of scepticism which they will acquire, that these adolescents have a chance of escaping obscurantism.'[2]

Although raised by some women's organisations, specifically Expressions Maghrébiennes au Feminin, the feminist issues sparked by the controversy were only a minor aspect of the public debate. This rigidity of approach and unquestioned assumption of cultural superiority also informs the French insistence on the desirability of spreading the immigrant population thinly. The central concept here is that of the 'threshold of tolerance' – a pseudo-scientific notion that the 'host' population can only be expected to accept a certain proportion of 'foreign' residents in any one area. This has been accepted across the political spectrum,[3] and the idea, though criticised by anti-racists, has survived more widely in the form of the rejection of imagined 'ghettos'. Like the 'threshold' concept, the refusal to countenance the formation of 'ghettos' is presented in progressive guise, as being in the interests of the people it rejects. But instead of focusing attention on the social conditions in which immigrants are forced to live and the cuts in housing, education and unemployment that affect them particularly, such an approach suggests that it is the very presence of immigrants which is the problem.*

* It is worth noting, perhaps, that this rejection of 'ghettoisation' does not extend to rejecting the squalid and unsavoury hostels in which immigrant workers are still housed.

Immigrants and immigration

The complexity of these issues can best be understood by considering who the 'immigrant' populations of France are and how these communities have developed. The term 'immigrant' is widely used in France, but is highly problematic and has the effect of emphasising the impermanence of the disparate communities it describes. The very fact of its currency emphasises how little acceptance there is among the white French population that there are now many different communities settled in France over several generations. There is no satisfactory concept, and hence no terminology for a community that falls between the 'immigrant' outsider and that of the assimilated French – only disputed terms to describe specific groups such as '*beurs*' (Parisian back-slang for Arab) or 'populations of immigrant origins'.

Thus, in France, the same term 'immigrant' is used to describe widely differing populations which, taken together, total nearly four and a half million people* out of a population of approximately 56 million, just under 7 per cent of the total. For years, people from various European countries – particularly Portugal, Italy and Spain, but also Belgium, Poland and Yugoslavia – have come to France for seasonal or more permanent work. A significant population has also arrived as refugees: recent asylum-seekers have come from South-East Asia, South America and the Middle East. Then there are those from the Overseas Departments of France (such as Guadeloupe, Martinique, French Guinea, etc.), who, while having full rights as French citizens, are in practice subjected to the most flagrant discrimination. Finally, there are large communities of Algerians, Moroccans and Tunisians (and to a lesser extent Indo-Chinese), whose presence, like that of the Martiniquans and Guadeloupans, is inextricably linked with France's colonial history.

The philosophy and strategies of French colonialism were, like the theories of French society, marked by the universalism of Enlightenment thinking. Hence, the French were more zealous in the export of their culture and language than the British, aiming at an integrated total population of a hundred million inhabitants within a national territory which extended over France and the colonies and formed, or was meant to form, an indissoluble unity. Assimilationist pressures were strong: commentators refer to the 'legendary capacity of the French to make foreigners into Frenchmen'.[5] However, such assimilation was, inevitably, on French terms and involved the renunciation

---

* The 1986 figures for 'immigrant' populations in France are: Portuguese (628,772), then Algerian (588,981), Italian (534,996), Spanish (441,514), Moroccan (385,796), Tunisian (172,615) and Turkish (117,353).[4]

of one's language, culture, customs, etc., which was particularly unacceptable to Muslims in North Africa.

Of all France's colonies, the one in which this dynamic – between a populous, largely Islamic society and a proselytising, settler colonialism – was played out most fully was Algeria. Geographically close, with a large French settler population which retained close ties to the mother country, Algeria lay at the heart of French colonial policy, which was strongly influenced by the fear of white settler secession. Thus, the future of the French colonial subject was always seen by the French as falling within a 'greater France', and systems of government were established, within the overall republican tradition, of a highly centralised state apparatus. Citizenship of greater France was clearly defined by the *'code de nationalité'*. On independence, though precise arrangements may have differed somewhat, the former colonial subject could choose either French nationality or that of the country of origin. Those who opted for French citizenship would obviously do so in the context of living and working within France.

In the recent past, large numbers of people have come to France for seasonal work in the vineyards and orchards and for general agricultural work – although the numbers have fallen by about 35 per cent since 1981, mainly because of mechanisation of the wine harvest. Today, the vast majority of immigrant workers in France (76 per cent) are manual workers, mostly in the construction and manufacturing industries. They therefore tend to live in urban and industrial areas such as the Ile de France area (around Paris), the Rhône-Alpes, Provence-Alpes-Côte d'Azur, the Nord-Pas-de-Calais and Lorraine. More than half (67 per cent) of immigrants living in France have settled in these regions.[6]

Immigration policies

Although the history of immigration to France (and racist violence associated with it) can be traced back through the nineteenth century, immigration really began to be systematised and regulated in the early years of the twentieth century. The first system of contracts for agricultural and mining workers was established between the French and Polish governments in 1908. At the same time, larger numbers of Algerians and Italians were also being recruited for industrial work. During the 1914-18 war, France looked to its colonies (especially North Africa and Indo-China) for special units of workers organised by the Ministry of Labour. From 1917 to 1940, foreigners had to carry an identity card, which became the basis on which they were regulated. The Ministry of the Interior kept centralised records, duplicates of those kept locally (all foreigners had to register with either the local police or the local town hall).

During the 1920s, the foreign population increased from the pre-1914 level of 2 per cent of the population to some 10 per cent. There was a massive demand for such labour because of French population losses during the war, the need to re-build devastated areas, the need for agricultural labour and to restart industry. Throughout this period, there was concern about the failure of the French population to reproduce itself and immigration (of people who, it was thought, could be assimilated) was encouraged.

The 1930s saw an increase in xenophobia and panic about foreigners, especially as war drew nearer. Police controls were tightened and record-keeping on immigrants further systematised and increased, until finally a powerful system of internal regulation was in place. As a contemporary critic remarked: 'France polices immigration but has no immigration policy.'[7]

At the end of the Second World War, it remained to the Left (sharing power with the Gaullists) to attempt to develop a coherent immigration strategy. In 1946, it set up a government agency, the National Office of Immigration (ONI) for that purpose. This had been a demand of organised labour (and the trade unions), to safeguard French workers and prevent them being undercut by cheap immigrant labour. Because the ONI functioned at intergovernmental level, certain minimum standards, levels of security, etc., for the migrant workers were built into the agreements it made with the sending countries. But, during the 1950s, many employers continued to recruit so-called 'clandestine' labour. For the ONI's bureaucracy was too cumbersome for private enterprise, which wanted workers as quickly as possible. The agreements operated by ONI, it should be noted, favoured white, European workers (recruitment centres were set up in Italy, Portugal, Yugoslavia, Spain and Morocco).[8] Such workers could integrate more easily into French society, but by the same token were not so readily exploitable. Why get involved in paying wages at the legal minimum and taxes on immigrant workers coming through the correct channels when they could be smuggled in, paid cash in hand as long as needed and quickly disposed of when unwanted? Such workers could, in any case, regularise their position after a time. Official policy connived with this – as one economic commentator put it (in the French equivalent of the *Financial Times*): 'Clandestine immigration has its uses, because if we kept to the strict application of international agreements, we would not have enough labour power.'[9] Thus, 'clandestine' immigration ran, at first, alongside official immigration, but eventually far outstripped it.*

In the immediate post-war period, the first workers to come in large

---

* By the 1960s, 'clandestine' immigration was built into the system, with only 23% of immigrants coming through ONI and 77% originating as 'clandestines'.

numbers, both officially and as 'clandestines', were the Algerians, immigration of whom into France had been gathering pace even before the Second World War. Algeria was, after all, the colony most closely linked to France, the scene of its most intense experiment to impose its own patterns and mores – if not on another culture as a whole – on a section of that society that would accept French dominance. Regarded as an extension of France (it was a *département*) lying just across the Mediterranean, it was used as a primary source of the labour needed for the new and growing French industries.

But the Second World War had not only changed France radically, it had also had a profound impact within Algeria, accelerating proletarianisation and giving an impetus to migration from the countryside. After the war, pressure grew for Algerian independence. At the same time, post-war Algerian migrants to France were quite different from their pre-war compatriots. They were more critical of the peasant society they had left behind and tended to stay longer in France. North African cafés in France were an important social focus and provided an organisational base for the new, secret political independence organisations, the Organisation Secrète (OS) and the Front de Libération National, and by the time Algeria's war of independence broke out, in 1954,[10] many had returned. Algerians now numbered some 12 per cent of the total foreign population – fewer than Italians, Spanish and Poles. Algerian migration was the most sensitive to the economic and political climate, and numbers continued to drop as this most bloody and bitter of wars was fought out.

But those Algerians who had, perforce, to remain in France from economic necessity were intensely vulnerable to a French society and polity that saw itself as betrayed by its own colonial offspring. They, ingratitude incarnate, became the butt of savage, racist antagonism. (For much of the war, many French conservatives had believed the ordinary Algerian to be, at heart, pro-French.)[11]

The violence used against them in France throughout this time was extreme – particularly if resistance appeared to be organised there. And just as there was a cross-over between Algerians in France working secretly for the liberation movement, so there was a cross-over between the *pieds noirs*, the violently pro-France white settlers, and layers of French officialdom. Thus, Papon, the chief of police in Paris in 1961, had served in the French colonial administration, including that of Algeria, in the late 1950s.[12]

Harassment, too, was extreme. Throughout 1961, as the war was coming to its climax, Algerians in Paris were subject to an evening curfew – a signal to police to stop anyone they took for Algerian in the streets. People were beaten. Some disappeared. Some died. But the most horrifying outrage of all was over the FLN rally on 17 October

1961. A series of marches in Paris – of many thousands, almost exclusively Algerians – was held to demand an end to the harassment and to the curfews, and independence for Algeria. What followed was unparalleled in recent French history. Some police drove demonstrators into the Seine, there to drown; some literally clubbed Algerians to death; others fired machine guns directly into the huge crowds. Eleven thousand people were arrested during the demonstration and held for several days. Between 140 to 200 people were known to have died; 400 were reported as missing, their fate unknown. This climactic savagery was followed in subsequent days by sporadic raids and violent beatings.

The response in France to these events was muted. Media reports were dominated by the police version in which the demonstrators were all portrayed as terrorists. The Left attempted, ineffectually, to draw attention to the brutal racism of the killings,[13] but was incapable, perhaps, of confronting both the terrorism of the government and the racism of its own constituency.[14]

From immigration to deportation

After independence, Algerian immigration became more sensitive to the needs of the Algerian domestic economy, and the Algerian government attempted to ensure minimum standards for its emigrants, insisting that Algerian workers should be found housing and a return-ticket if they were to go to work in France. Given the new constraints on Algerian immigration, France turned to Morocco (an increase of 13 per cent in 1965) and Tunisia (an increase of 11 per cent between 1962 and 1966). And from the mid-1960s on, the sources of immigration were widened to include Turkey, Portugal, Yugoslavia and Mali, Mauritania and Senegal.

By the late 1960s, racist prejudices were feeding on the exploitation of immigrants who, in the politically polarised situation of that period, took up unskilled, low-paid jobs. In doing so, they bore the burden of the modernisation of French industry and, in many ways, shielded white French workers, by buffering the impact of fundamental changes in the nature of employment. Nor did the Left or the labour movement act in any way to counter the growth of prejudice or racism.

Trade unions (which were divided along political lines and, as a body, lacked overall cohesion) tended to recruit among the more highly qualified French workers. Little unionisation at all was available to the low-skilled, and immigrants were regarded as vulnerable to management pressure. They were seen as a threat – the Algerian war had shown how dramatically and decisively French culture and society had been rejected, and this had affected the consciousness of the Left no less than the Right. Claims to class and international solidarity could easily slip into another variant of the assimilationism that rejected all those who were not cultural copies of the French, while immigrants themselves could be hypothesised as a threat to working-class unity. In the view of Georges Marchais, general secretary of the Communist Party since the early 1970s, immigration was a means of exerting pressure on the working class in order to divide it. It was, therefore, in the interests of French workers to demand equal rights for 'immigrants' so as to protect their own living standards.[15]

In this climate, the large CP-dominated union, the CGT, supported government policies to end immigration. Assimilation and control were the themes of a major 1969 government report on immigration. Measures to restrict immigration were to be balanced by attempts to improve immigrants' social conditions – particularly housing. What followed throughout the 1970s, under a series of rightist governments, was a succession of increasingly restrictive immigration measures, coupled with an ever more virulent campaign against the 'clandes-tines'. (France, as elsewhere in Europe, was going through a major economic downturn during this period.) Not that this was achieved without cost to the government, for, increasingly, immigrant workers' political activity was based on their acceptance that they would stay in France (with struggles being fought over housing and discrimination as well) and considerable agitation followed the first such package of immigration control measures in 1972. In the same year, the government was also forced to grant the passage of a law against racism* and certain rights to representation in the workplace for immigrants.

The issue of race and immigration became, however, increasingly explosive with, in the summer of 1973, a massive outburst of racist violence, lasting over months, against Algerians. Starting in Marseil-le, it spread across all France. This prompted the Algerian government to suspend immigration. By the time of the presidential elections of 1974, immigration was a central political issue, readily exploited by such groups as the extreme right Ordre Nouveau, which built up the 'clandestine' immigrant worker into the major threat facing France. On taking office, the new (right-wing) government acted immediately to halt all further immigration – prompting a wave of protest and hunger strikes among immigrants and anti-racists throughout the country. The pressure against immigrants continued throughout the 1970s, with a short lived attempt to prevent family reunification, an unsuccessful policy of induced repatriation and, most significantly,

---

* The law contains provisions against discrimination in employment, housing, provision of services and incitement to racial hatred. The law is poorly enforced, and proof under it is extremely difficult. The cases brought most often are those concerned with incitement.

regular campaigns to deport the 'clandestines'. Even as primary immigration was ending, the 'clandestine' began to be represented as the symbol of all that was 'undesirable', a charge on public funds, a threat to public order (rather like the 'dangerous classes' of earlier times) and a numerical threat to French national identity. Culture, values, life-style, language, all were different. Unassimilable in the sense simply of being not French, the 'clandestine' had, ultimately, to be purged from the body politic. It is perhaps not untoward to see, in the Islamic culture and mores of the North African immigrants who were the butt of the most vicious racism, a reminder to France of its recent war with the representatives of another Islamic culture; its earlier failure to engulf and assimilate. Whatever the reason, anti-Arab racism found a ready hold in the French mind and in French society. Taking a leaf out of Ordre Nouveau's book, the right-wing governments of the 1970s used the figure of the 'clandestine' to imply that all immigrants (or people who might look like immigrants) could be illegal or engaged in criminal activity. And it is at this point that the hitherto 'clandestine' workforce, smuggled in with the tacit conni-vance of employers and government, becomes transmogrified into the illegal. Conversely, all migrants were now stereotyped as illegals and/or engaged in criminal activity. Hence, in a French variant of the British sus laws, police harassment in the form of both systematic and random identity checks was thus legitimised, while reinforcing the popular equation of Arab-immigrant-criminal.

Government policy reached its apogee in the 'Bonnet' law (Bonnet was the government minister whose brainchild the new law was) of 1980. Under this, deportation became a cinch. People who had lived and worked in France for years, who had entered the country when the authorities looked on 'clandestine' immigration with a blind eye – even minors, even people whose own children were French citizens – were rounded up and turfed out. At their height, the deportations were running at around 4,000 a year. The worst excesses of the law were, it is true, curbed when a socialist government under Mitterrand finally took over from the right-wing government of Giscard d'Estaing in 1981. Under Mitterrand, restrictions (dating back to 1939) on the political activities of non-French nationals were also repealed, making it easier for immigrants to organise politically, so that, by 1985, more than 4,000 such associations had been formed.[16] And there was a brief cessation of pressure on the 'illegals' (whose status was, in any case, always subject to political expediency). Nonetheless, the increasingly hysterical racism of the 1970s – agitated by the far right, virtually uncontested by the Left, promulgated by successive governments, promoted by the media and endorsed by popular sentiment – had achieved its effect. The stage was set for the triumphal re-entry into the mainstream of French politics of the racist Right, the FN, in the early 1980s. And after its electoral breakthrough in the municipal elections of 1983, the Front has largely set the racial agenda in French political life.

All this is not to say, however, that immigrant workers and their families have been passive in the face of the racism and hostility that have confronted them. There is not space here to go into all the bitter struggles, against employment discrimination, immigration policies, police harassment, municipal racism, that have been waged over the years. But, the crucial issue over which the most violent battles have been fought – not least, because France prides itself on not yielding to the British 'malaise' of creating immigrant ghettos – is housing. And it is to this aspect of struggle that we now turn.

The battle over housing

Housing demonstrates as clearly, perhaps, as any other single issue the determination of government and employers to extract systematically maximum value at minimum cost from immigrant workers. It is in the application of housing policy that one can see most clearly the twin poles of French official thinking – on the one hand, to keep what is non-French at arm's length from French society; on the other, to render it invisible, to dilute any possible contamination, by spreading it as thinly as possible. Hence, the 'threshold of tolerance' theory mentioned earlier. Hence, also, the fact that French policies on housing have evolved quite distinct from those elsewhere in Europe (though, as in Germany, since 1984, possession of satisfactory housing conditions determines family reunification).

There is less public housing in France than in Britain: inner-city areas are being yuppified, while working-class estates and public housing are on the outskirts. Until relatively recently, immigrant workers have occupied the most marginal housing conditions. The squalid shanty towns or bidonvilles surrounding the major cities of France, where large numbers of immigrant workers lived in the 1950s, 1960s and 1970s, have now disappeared. They had grown up initially because of the desperate housing needs of the immigrant workers, the closed nature of French society to accommodate them in any other way, and the completely inadequate official provision of special hostels. But, with their connotations of ghetto-like concentrations of immigrants, they were a ready target for official action – in a way which also gave vent to official racism, as, for example, in 1961, when bidonvilles around Paris were raided and besieged by police. Today, large numbers of immigrants, single men, still live like guestworkers in overcrowded hostels with inadequate facilities. Most hostels are owned by Sonacotra (Société Nationale de Construction de Logement pour les Travailleurs), a national organisation set up in 1956 to build lodgings for workers and financed with public and private money.[17] Originally intended for Algerians, it was later extended to all immigrant workers. In 1975, funding methods were changed, rents increased and many people were forced to leave. A series of rent strikes were organised, which became a focus of political activity and mobilisation.

Hostels have often been a target for the terrorist Right: in autumn 1988, right-wing bombers from the Parti National Français et Européen (PNFE) made a series of attacks on immigrant workers living in them. (Links were later discovered between the PNFE and the right-wing police union, the Fédération Indépendante de la Police (FPIP). One person was killed, many injured and everyone living in hostels felt endangered.[18]

Another avenue to housing taken by many immigrant workers is squatting. An organised movement has developed with many squats run by 'committees of the badly housed'. Recent struggles have taken place with the council of Paris over the possession of derelict buildings now being squatted. For many of these are situated near the newly built and prestigious Opera House, in an area ripe for redevelopment. But the squatters have refused to move until they were properly rehoused. In one case, the owner requested the prefecture of police to send in riot squads to evict the squatters – but this was too much, even for the Paris police, who refused.[19] Then, some days later at 3am, residents were violently woken by tear-gas cylinders being thrown by masked men into the building. A private commando raid had been carried out to terrorise them into leaving. Or, again, when a group of West African families squatted in newly built public housing in the 11th arrondissement, the right-wing Paris council attempted to drive them out by cutting off water and electricity. The families held out for several months, in appalling conditions, until the Department of Health ordered services to be restored.[20]

The problem is exacerbated because low rent public housing is so scarce. In Paris, for instance, it amounts to only 8 per cent of total housing. People whose income is uncertain cannot obtain public housing because of city regulations which, for a small flat costing 2,600f a month, require proof of a stable income of 8,000f a month. So, many poor people are driven into the exploitative and often squalid private sector. A study in 1987 found that 40 per cent of lodgings without running water were occupied by families of foreign origin.[21]

Nor is it only lack of a good steady income that has kept immigrant workers out of public housing. In the early years, they were delibe-rately excluded from subsidised housing, the 'habitations à loyer modéré' (HLM). They were only able to gain access to this type of accommodation when French people left it to buy their own property, and did not move into HLM in large numbers until after 1976. Racism still ensured, however, that they went mainly to housing estates which had been abandoned because of bad conditions or inconvenient location.

But subsequent attempts to improve conditions in the estates were used by HLM associations to encourage French families to return on the basis of the 'threshold of tolerance' theory, by which immigrants were to be scattered as thinly as possible among the indigenous population.[22] In pursuit of this 'balance', many housing managers try to force out immigrants from HLM housing, often by allowing the fabric and surroundings of the building to deteriorate. In Montfermeil, right-wing mayor Pierre Bernard has refused to spend any money on the Bosquets housing estate he inherited from his Communist predecessors. The estate comprises 1,590 flats, 80-95 per cent of which are inhabited by immigrants, some thirty nationalities. There are no facilities on this estate; even public transport is non-existent. Bernard has refused to improve the estate until he can bring in more white French families.[23]

The estate of Gennevilliers-Port to the north of Paris is a similar case. When the management of this HLM increased rents for the second year running in 1986, the tenants refused to pay. Since then, the rent strike has become institutionalised, even though the tenants are cut off from the outside world with no services. Many of them (some 600) are from Morocco, Algeria, Senegal and Mali. It has so far proved impossible to enforce court orders against the management who, since 1984, have been using government grants to improve their properties, then charging highly inflated rents.*

However, nothing illustrates so clearly how housing is deemed to be pivotal to the race issue, on the Left and on the Right, as the recent events in Lyon. In early October, in a suburb with a mainly immigrant population (Vaulx en Velin), violent rioting broke out after a motor cycle pillion passenger died in a collision (believed to have been deliberately caused) with a police car. Indeed, what happened in Vaulx en Velin crystallises many of the themes covered here. Vaulx, like many similar suburbs was a typical 1970s high-rise, urban development of, in Serge July's words, 'riotous concrete and Taylorist planning', into which were concentrated the poor and socially deprived.[24] The ever-present fear of the many estates like Vaulx turning into ghettos prompted the socialist government of the 1980s into a spending

---

* There have, too, been political corruption scandals around HLM housing. In the 20th arrondissement of Paris, an area where many North African people live, right-wing politician Didier Barhani was discovered to be packing empty HLM flats with his political supporters, while immigrants remained unhoused following a spate of racist arsons in the area.

programme to transform them. No doubt, the government's mind was also concentrated by the 1981 riots in the same area, to which the solution was seen as a massive and genuine improvement in housing conditions (unlike anything that would be even contemplated in Britain). This was a view subsequently endorsed by Harlem Désir of SOS Racisme, who opined that the malaise in such suburbs could be alleviated by 'repairing the lifts' rather than 'shouting about Le Pen'.[25] (Désir, however, is not of the generation that took to the streets of Lyon on this occasion.)

The rioting broke out the day after the latest phase in this ambitious programme was opened. They had built the homes, laid out the lawns, set up shops and even fabricated a library. Literally, everything in the garden was rosy. But they had failed to stop the constant police harassment of young people (police 'mishaps' had caused the deaths of at least eleven 'immigrants' over the past ten years) or to provide them with the jobs that would keep them off the streets. All the authorities seemed to be interested in was to extend the threshold of French 'tolerance', from housing into society, from generation unto generation.

The rise and rise of the FN

If the youths of Lyon have reacted so forcefully to the cultural exclusion, social segregation and economic irrelevance visited on them, what of those who have identified themselves so effectively as the true upholders of French values, the FN? The dramatic rise of the FN since the early 1980s, has been one of the most significant developments in French politics. Emerging during a period of deep long-term economic and social change, it has been at one level part cause, at another part effect, of France's growing racial polarisation.

The FN stagnated for many years – between 1972, when Le Pen became leader, until 1983, when it gained municipal seats in a by-election pact with the right-wing UDF-RPR coalition. In 1984, Le Pen, along with nine other FN candidates, won seats in the European parliament. The FN has continued to go from strength to strength, winning thirty-five seats in 1986 to the French National Assembly, and, in the presidential elections of 1988, polling over 14 per cent of the vote against Mitterand. Since its 1983 breakthrough, the FN has moved skilfully and swiftly to exploit the political space abandoned to it by the Left's failure to challenge racism (including its own) and the established Right's internal disarray. From 1983, politicians of both the Left and Right have attempted to defend an increasingly belea-guered economy by scapegoating immigrants. In the process, they have fuelled a racism that the FN was poised to exploit. For example, it set the agenda for the passage of the Pasqua law (1986) which further tightened immigration control, and was introduced as a measure against 'clandestine immigration and imported delinquency'.[26]

The one or two ostensibly anti-racist measures undertaken by the socialist government under Mitterrand, such as allowing immigrants to form political associations, promising housing reforms, etc., do not belie its essentially racist immigration policies. Government social policies, by which significant powers have been devolved to the local level (the opposite of recent British experience) have also enabled extreme right-wing municipalities to refuse housing and education to 'immigrants'.

The simple fact of the FN's success has acted to legitimate it further; its support comes from all sections of society. According to the European parliament's recent report on racism, it has influence among the police, judiciary and armed forces, and a growing following in university and academic circles.[27] It has, moreover, been aided by the collapse of the organised Left – taking over from the declining PCF even in its former industrial heartlands. Such inroads have been made easier in that the PCF, on occasion, has accommodated popular racism – most notoriously when the Communist mayor at Vitry gave orders to bulldoze a hostel where immigrant workers were living.[28]

Thus, when Le Pen speaks out against the 'Islamicisation of France' – he claims France is in imminent danger of becoming an Islamic nation – he stokes the fears and uncertainties of ordinary French people caught in the trough of post-industrial change. And as for his claim to speak for the working man, against capital and the 'foreigners', the ground, as we have seen, had already been prepared by the PCF.

Nor have the specifically anti-racist organisations, such as MRAP and SOS Racisme, had much success in combating either the FN or the wider vein of French racism from which it draws vigour. The oldest organisation, MRAP, it is true, does work at a local level, with 'immigrant' associations, offering a legal advice service and attempting to get the 1972 anti-discrimination law enforced. But the largest and best known is SOS Racisme, which was set up in the mid-1980s, and has held rallies and demonstrations, campaigning on the slogan of 'Touche pas à mon pote' ('Don't touch my pal'). Its emphasis on changing personal, individual attitudes has hampered any closer or tougher fight against the institutions that perpetuate and engender racism. And, broadly speaking, it sees the solution to racism as a variant of assimilation. The definition of French culture, the interpretation of French universalist and rationalist values should be broadened so as to make room for immigrant youth. Hence, Muslim girls should be enticed away from separate (Muslim) schools into French schools, by being allowed to wear the veil, so as to be inculcated with the values of the Enlightenment – and then, in Désir's words, 'Jeans will eventually win over the chador.'[29]

Accompanying the rise of the FN has come an escalation not only in racial violence against the Arabs, but in racial intimidation of the Jews. The recent desecration of the Jewish cemetery at Carpentras, where headstones were daubed with swastikas, graves opened up and the corpse of one recently buried old man mutilated, was only the most flagrant among a number of similar incidents. Liberal public opinion was outraged, the press was united in condemnation and a huge, silent march of protest was headed by no less a person than the French president.

Anti-Semitism has a long and deep tradition in France, surfacing most notably in the response to German overlordship during the Second World War. Under the Vichy regime's ready collusion with the Nazis, Jews were stigmatised and thousands deported. Remembrance of this, and the swift collapse of military resistance to the German take-over, touches a raw nerve in French consciousness. And, for that reason, perhaps, it is not a memory that is opened up: at official remembrance days, the experiences of Jewish deportees from France are hardly dwelt upon.

On the other hand, the Resistance and its fight against anti-Semitism have been mythologised as the true expression of the French nation. Thus, today, activity to combat anti-Semitism has been privileged over other forms of anti-racist activity in France. Hence the outrage over Carpentras; hence, too, the fear at the resurgence of widely diffused anti-Semitism that has never been properly contested.*

Anti-Semitism threatens the image of enlightened France. Anti-Arab racism gives the lie to France's assimilationist creed. Stemming, as it does (principally), from the trauma of the Algerian war of independence, it replicates the savagery of that episode in French history. It is not accidental that areas of France where racial violence (and FN support) occur most frequently are also areas of high *pied noir* (French ex-colonial) settlement, such as the Côte d'Azur. Some of the aggressors are known to have fought in Algeria. Or, again, the way that these attacks have been mounted mirrors tactics used by the French in the Algerian war. We have already mentioned the commando raids on the Sonacotra hostels and the bombing campaign of 1988. (Hostel wardens themselves are often ex-soldiers who fought in Algeria and institute a strict, racist regime of discipline.)

Such cases often display an extra degree of savagery. For example,

---

* As we write, the issue of the culpability of officials of the Vichy regime has been side-stepped once again. Attempts to call some of those responsible for the deportations to account have been shelved by the complications of correct judicial procedure: less perhaps to safeguard a few old men than France's own amour propre.[30]

a security guard at Marseille station tortured Neji Sayah (from Tunisia) by taking him to a cellar where he was physically assaulted, forced to drink a mixture of wine and salt, poisoned with tear gas and thrown into a gully. The torture treatment was similar to one used in the Foreign Legion.[31]

Nor is the casual disregard for life (evidenced in France's war with Algeria) absent from the way 'immigrants' in France have been killed – merely because they are Arabs and deserve to be punished, or, like one youngster shot in the back, because he broke a window. Some incidents may be less savage, but equally macabre: take, for instance, the pageant on the theme of the Algerian war organised by ex-combatants in the small town of Montregard. Among the activities was a mock 'chasse à la Fatma' (hunt of Algerian women, in racist parlance). Virtually the whole community witnessed this or took part.[32]

So, if there is one element of the racist Right attempting to fight the Second World War over again, mounting a poisonous and threatening campaign against the Jews, there is another attempting to replay the Algerian war. And both tributaries meet in the FN, symbolised in the figure of ex-Algerian combatant, paratrooper Jean Marie Le Pen. The FN's anti-Semitism is notorious, as are the links between this organisation and anti-Arab violence.*

Is Le Pen's the authentic voice of a France that claims it is heir to the ideas of liberty, equality and fraternity engendered by the Enlightenment? Or do those ideas mask a culture that is becoming irrational, exclusivist and deeply racist?

References

1   P. Legrain, 'Musulmans en France ou Musulmans de France?', *Esprit* (Octobre 1986).
2   Interview with Harlem Désir in *Libération* (21 October 1989).
3   C. Lloyd, ' What is the French CP up to?', *Race & Class* (Spring 1981).
4   M. Tribalat, 'Chronique de l'immigration', *Population* (January-February 1989).
5   Martin Schain, *Immigration and Politics* (1990).
6   MRAP, *La verité sur les immigrés en France* (1987).

* There is a good deal of evidence associating the FN with racial violence. In some cases, perpetrators found guilty of racist acts are shown to have been ex-members of the FN who then moved on to more extreme organisations. In particular, links were found between the FN and the people who bombed the Sonacotra hostels for immigrants on the Côte d'Azur. One of the first people arrested for this crime was Gilbert Hervochan, who was well-known as a right-wing personality, and had been an FN candidate in the municipal elections in Nice in 1983. The man who shot an Arab youngster for breaking a window was an FN local councillor. And an FN official in Marseille, André Lambert, was found guilty of shooting Laurent Zabel, a young man of North African origin – for which he received a suspended sentence.[33]

7   W. Oualid, 'Pour une politique de l'immigration en France', *Esprit* (July 1939).
8   M. Bideberry, 'Immigration et techniques de Recruitement', *Economie et Humanisme* (Sept/Oct 1969). Bideberry was the first president of the ONI.
9   J.M. Jeanneney, *Les Echos* (29 Mars 1966).
10 At the outbreak of war more than one million *'pieds noirs'* were living in Algeria. The other major group involved in the maintenance of French power were the Harkis, Algerian auxilliary soldiers in the French army recruited after 1957. They were sometimes attached to the civil administration, sometimes charged with maintaining order in the countryside. After independence, some 80,000 - 100,000 left for a very uncertain future in France. See F. Guidice, *Têtes de Turcs en France* (Paris, 1989).
11 V. Kiernan, *European empires from conquest to collapse, 1815-1960* (London, 1982).
12 Maurice Papon had earlier , under the Vichy Government, special responsibility for Jewish affairs in Bordeaux; in other words organising deportations of Jews to Germany. M. Slitinsky, *L'affaire Papon* (A. Moreau, 1983).
13 *Bulletin Municipal Officiel de la Ville de Paris* (27 Octobre 1961).
14 M. Levine, *Les Ratonnades d'Octobre, un meutre collectif à Paris en 1961* (Ramsay, 1985).
15 G. Marchais, 'L'Immigration en France', *Cahiers du Communisme* (11 Novembre 1965).
16 C. Wihtol de Wenden, 'Les Immigrés et la politique: insertion et participation', *Les Cahiers de l'Orient* (3, 1986).
17 Sonacotra was originally funded by FAS and Credit Foncier and today has 340 establishments, 71,000 single rooms and 2,000 family lodgings, *Libération* (10 Juin 1989).
18 The FPIP is also very close to the FN; in November 1989, Le Pen sent a personal note of support to FPIP candidates in professional elections, *Le Nouvel Observateur* (12-18 Avril 1990) and *Libération* (10 Octobre 1989).
19 *Libération* (5 and 21 Août 1989).
20 *Libération* (4 Août 1989).
21 Survey by the Conseil Economique et Sociale, cited in Guidice, op. cit., p. 38.
22 M. Blanc, 'Immigration housing in France: from hovel to hostel to low-cost flats, *New Community* (Summer 1985).
23 *Libération* (2 Novembre 1989).
24 S. July, 'Nightmare in a place of dreams', *Guardian* (19 October 1990).
25 Television interview, L'Heure de Verité, quoted in *Libération* (20 Août 1987).
26 Minister of the Interior in a television interview March 1986, quoted in C-V Marie, 'Entre economie et politique: le clandestin, une figure sociale à geometrie variable', *Pouvoirs* (No 47, 1988).
27 European Parliament Committee of Inquiry into the Rise of Racism and Fascism in Europe, *Report* (rapporteur Glyn Ford) (Strasbourg, 1990).
28 Lloyd, op. cit.
29 *Le Monde* (9 Janvier 1990)
30 Mitterrand 'holds up trials of war criminals', *Guardian* (22 October 1990).
31 *Libération* (30 Juin 1989).
32 *Libération* (25 Août 1988).
33 *Libération* (29 Juin 1988, 27 Février, 6 Mars, 3 and 4 Mai 1989).

FREDDY MERCKX and LIZ FEKETE

Belgium: the racist cocktail

Much of Belgium's history predates its formation as a neutral nation state, under the auspices of the great European powers, in 1831. The provinces that comprise it were famous in medieval times for the rich and precious quality of their manufactures: the fine woollens of Ghent, the stained glass and glowing tapestries of Flanders, the finely wrought metal work of Dinant. Antwerp was one of the earliest and greatest commercial cities, while the fertile, reclaimed lands of Flanders and Zeeland fed a growing population in what were the largest cities of northern Europe. And the area formed part of the arena for the religio-political (Catholic-Protestant) wars that racked European history. It is a region that has always been of strategic importance in European conflicts – whether between Spain and the Netherlands (with Britain also bent on retaining a measure of influence and control) or between France and Germany.

Neither a natural geographic, nor even a single linguistic, entity, Belgium was, in effect, carved out of the territory left over after centuries of European upheaval; as a buffer zone almost. Bounded by the Netherlands to the north, Germany to the south and France to the north-west, it was occupied by Germany during both world wars.

But the centuries of conflict in and around this region, of Dutch and French overlordship, have left their mark, principally in the division of Belgium into two main linguistic zones, with Dutch the official language of the north (Flanders) and French the official language of the south (Wallonia). Brussels, located in the north and the hub of

---

* Freddy Merckx is a medical practitioner living in Brussels, who is active in the anti-racist movement there. *Liz Fekete* who lives in London was a founding member of Anti-Fascist Action.

Race & Class, 32(3), 1991

much international bureaucracy including that of the European Community (EC), is bilingual. There is also a small German-speaking region on the German border.

Historically, French was the language of government and the elite; the Flemings of the agricultural north were the underdogs. From its formation, Belgium underwent its own industrial revolution, aided by the country's huge reserves of coal (practically its only natural resource), which had been exploited since the seventeenth century. By the mid-nineteenth century, too, Belgium's railway network was in place, giving rapid, easy transit to Germany, France, Netherlands and, with a sea link, to Britain. Densely-populated (as it has been throughout its history), Belgium had a labour-force ready to hand for the iron works, the paper mills, the cotton, woollen and linen factories, the new chemical plants. A 'paradise for capitalists' was how Marx saw it.[1]

But whereas the French-speaking south was the early recipient of prosperity, and the north the more backward, underdeveloped region – a divide compounded by the linguistic inequity (leading, in its turn, to social and educational injustice) – today, it is the south whose traditional industries are declining, and the north which is becoming the location for the new. All of which has simply added another twist to the historic animosity between the Dutch-speaking north and the French-speaking south (today some 57 per cent of Belgium's indigenous population are Dutch speakers, some 42 per cent French speaking, and less than 1 per cent German speaking).[2]

It is this, above all, which has shaped Belgium's political development, and its structures of government – which have become in theory more devolved and in practice more bureaucratic. Thus, in addition to the national government, every region (i.e., Flanders, Wallonia and Brussels) has its own executive and legislative body with considerable jurisdiction over issues such as education. All the main political parties are split into both French and Flemish sections, as are the union federations, with the language issue frequently overriding other political considerations. While the north mainly supports the conservative Christian Social Party and the nationalist Volksunie, the French-speaking south votes predominantly socialist.[3]

Despite increases in unemployment in the 1980s,* and the imposition under a succession of coalition governments of stringent austerity measures involving large cuts in public expenditure, Belgium is, and remains, an extremely prosperous country. It is a prosperity that also owes not a little to its use, post-war, of migrant labour from, first, southern Europe, and then Third World countries like Morocco

---

* Belgium's economy is dependent on external trade and thus immediately vulnerable to fluctuations in the international market; moreover, its heavy industry is in decline.

or Tunisia.

It could be said that, if Belgium acted as a buffer in Europe, the migrant worker has been the buffer in Belgium. For, in this most fissiparous of western European nations, it is the Third World migrant who is the anti-figure against which the others can cohere; it is the Third World migrant who does the jobs no longer wanted by the better-off Belgians; the migrant worker who, first and foremost, absorbs the shock of unemployment in declining industries; the migrant who keeps them going at as little cost to the employer and the state as possible; the Third World migrant who can be scapegoated for economic decline. And, as befits a nation which stands between the two giants of France and Germany, the system of controls over migrants, as well as the theories about them, bear traces of both French- and German-style practice. They have been made into a cocktail, though, that it is all Belgium's own.

At present, out of Belgium's 9.9 million population, just under 9 per cent are of foreign origin (868,757 was the actual figure as at January 1989).* Some 30 per cent of these live in Brussels (where foreigners are around one-quarter of the total population); just over 40 per cent in Wallonia (where they are 11 per cent of the total population), and nearly 30 per cent in Flanders (4 per cent of the total). But, there are foreigners and foreigners. A sharp distinction is made between those of EEC origin (some 62 per cent of the total foreign population) together with the personnel freely brought in by multinational corporations and agencies (Austrians, Swiss, Americans) and the Turkish, Tunisian or Moroccan migrant worker. While the former enjoy the same social status and privilege as the Belgian population, the latter experience sustained, institutionalised racism diffused throughout Belgium's bewildering variety of official bodies. It is they who are the focus of this article.

Interestingly, few migrants are from Zaire, Belgium's former colonial possession, which it dealt with so brutally and abandoned so bloodily and abruptly in 1960. What does connect the present to that past, however, is the residue of a racism which expressed itself in colonial terms in sheer despotic savagery (the Congo was King Leopold's personal fiefdom); in forced labour, food taxes, floggings, mutilation and murder. The extent of Belgian malpractices, the sheer indifference to black life, shocked even the other colonial powers. Today that racism is characterised by:
– an indifference to any concept of integration except that of complete assimilation to Belgian culture (naturalisation depends on this);
– a refusal to make any except the most minimal social provision for

---

* Of the different foreign communities, the Italians are the largest group (27.7 per cent of the total foreign population) followed by the Moroccans (15.63 per cent), the French (15.58 per cent) and the Turks (9.1 per cent).

migrant workers and their families (their only right is to work as cheap labour);
– an absence of any democratic rights for them;
– an absence of any training or education for them;
– overt segregation in education and housing;
– police harassment, often of a most brutal nature;
– hostility to any expression of their values or culture (especially Islam).
And, of course, a widespread, popular belief in the innate inferiority of non-white people which endorses any and every action taken against them.

Thus, for example, the children of migrant workers born in Belgium do not have any right to Belgian nationality; they are still 'foreign'. (It is a rather more sophisticated variant of the British National Front's view that a 'cat born in a kipper box doesn't become a kipper'.) Only if one parent has Belgian nationality does a child have the right to it – a change in the law which itself was not effected till 1985. Thus, in 1981, for example, just over 36 per cent of 'foreigners' were actually born in Belgium. It is a status which can, and does, have severe consequences for second-generation youth who are, by this token, subject to much of the repressive apparatus aimed at controlling and, latterly, excluding, non-white foreigners.

History of immigration policy

Initially, under Belgium's original constitution (which also guaranteed its neutrality), resident foreigners were to enjoy, by and large, the same freedoms as native Belgians. It was a liberalism of approach (in the old sense) that was to continue, with certain brief exceptions, throughout the remainder of the nineteenth century and into the early part of the twentieth. Indeed, at first, administrative and legislative control of both Belgians and non-Belgians developed side by side. Thus, under the German occupation of 1914-18 (which devastated Belgium) identity cards were introduced on identical terms for native and non-native. It is, perhaps, not surprising that the occupying forces should make no distinction between the two, but the same system continued post-war until the early 1930s, as Martens has shown.[4]

In the looming crisis of that period came something of a turning point. By a decree of 1933, a special identity card was introduced for foreigners and, for the first time, the policing of foreigners was implemented. For Jewish and anti-fascist refugees were already beginning to flee to Belgium: throughout the 1930s, tens of thousands would attempt to enter, those who made it being put to work in the factories and mills of Belgian industry. As numbers increased, so did the measures of control: the introduction of work permits for the first time in 1936 was followed, in 1939 and on the very eve of war, with draconian measures aimed at those who had entered 'illegally'. A new crime had been born – illegal immigration. Special centres were set up for Jews, the aim being to trace and deport them as rapidly as possible. Anti-Semitism flourished, abetted by quasi-fascist organisations such as the Catholic 'Rexists' in the south and certain sections of the Flemish nationalist movement, such as the Vlaams National Verbond (VNV).

Flemish nationalists had, in 1914-18, collaborated with the Germans, in the hope of ridding themselves of the yoke of Wallonian dominance. Now they, like their southern counterparts, were ready to collaborate for the greater cause of fascism. 'My attitude is not inspired by anti-Semitism or racism', declared Romsée, a member of the VNV, 'but I hold the view that the percentage of foreigners has exceeded the legal limit and that self-defence for the benefit of the people is necessary . . . Too many Jews have already come into our country. If Jewish immigration is not stopped, anti-Semitism will grow in our country as well, as people defend themselves.'[5]

The tenor of pre-war policy towards 'foreigners' can be illustrated by the fact that the same man, Robert Foy, head of security and responsible for the policing of 'aliens', remained in that post all during the German occupation, as well as after the war, until his death in 1958.

Under the German occupation, the VNV, along with other pre-war fascist groups, actively collaborated. The VNV, for example, set up local militia units and the 1,000-strong anti-Bolshevik League to fight in Russia. Thousands of Jews were deported – 25,000 to Auschwitz alone.[6] (Though if collaboration was readily embraced by some, so too was the underground resistance movement, whose strength, though mainly in Brussels and Wallonia, was not confined to those regions).

In the immediate post-war period, Belgium's economy recovered comparatively quickly, the motor for its recovery being once again the exploitation of its coal reserves. Immediately after the war, German prisoners of war (about 64,000) were forced to work in the mines, then, around 1946-7, their places were taken by some 70,000 Italian workers. Throughout the 1950s, and in the heyday of their productivity, the mines continued to use foreign labour, from Italy, Greece and Spain. With the 1960s came a decline in the profitability of the older mines in the south, but also an expansion in processing and manufacturing industry. Employers began to look further afield for sources of cheap labour, to Morocco and Turkey, where people were recruited directly from the countryside in special campaigns sponsored by the Belgian government. By this time, pre-war legislation aimed at controlling refugees had become the core of post-war legislation (passed in 1952) directed at migrant workers. Its aim was not so much to limit numbers as to retain control over migrant workers by reserving to the state fairly wide and arbitrary powers of expulsion. If, for example, a migrant's presence was deemed a threat or a nuisance to public safety or the country's economy, he could be ordered, without right of appeal, to leave. He would also have to leave if his employer refused to renew his work permit.

By the 1970s, migrant workers were working as domestic labour, in catering, on public transport, in the unglamorous jobs in health and medical care. Many had begun to settle and bring in their families – albeit living on the margins of Belgian society, in the poorest areas, virtually segregated from the wider community, their every step dogged by police and officialdom. They were strictly confined to the secondary labour market, subject to low wages, poor working conditions and frequent lay-offs. To this day, a foreign worker is barred by statute from any kind of public service or government employment, whether police officer or park-keeper, government clerk or railway guard. It has been their function to shore up and keep profitable as long as possible industries in decline, or supply a quick, ready-made labour force for industrial expansion.

But Belgium's economy experienced the same fall in the early 1970s as elsewhere in Europe. By 1974, primary immigration had virtually ceased, but this, as in Britain, did not stop racist politicians of all hues, from crying out against it. The 'increases' in 'immigration' that were pointed to were not, of course, in numbers of people entering, but increases in the so-called foreign population, of migrant workers' children born in Belgium, the entry of wives, etc.

At about the same time, however (from 1970 on), a wave of protest among students and young people swept the universities and colleges; the cause was a severe restriction on foreign students that had been proposed by the Justice Ministry. Some students went on hunger strike, others demonstrated and stopped work. The campaign swelled into a movement demanding legal rights and recognised status for foreigners – even as the Right was calling, ever more vehemently, for a further clamp-down. What the Right wanted was a law that would extend and incorporate all the ad hoc, piecemeal ministerial enactments and measures that had been multiplying unchecked over previous years. Out of this increasingly polarised situation emerged an apparent compromise that barely masked an ever more repressive policy. The anti-racist law as proposed did contain some worthwhile provisions – about the right to family reunification, about abrogating the hitherto legal right of local administrations to restrict the numbers of 'foreigners' in their areas.

However, by the time the law was enacted – it was blocked for something like two years, from 1978 to 1980, and only passed after mass anti-racist demonstrations – it was being undermined by developments elsewhere. Justice Minister Gol was to endorse the 'threshold of tolerance' theory, which held that foreigners should be dispersed throughout the 'host' population: below a certain percentage their presence was tolerable and would not give rise to problems; above, and it became intolerable. Not surprisingly, no action would be taken against those boroughs which had so assiduously been practising the theory, refusing to register (and therefore allow a right of residence to) 'foreigners'. And, the anti-racist law still retained the state's power of arbitrary expulsion and deportation, without right of appeal.

Meanwhile, under a ministerial circular of November 1977, new directives had been issued concerning family reunification. As these were strictly confidential, it was difficult to the point of absurdity for a would-be family member to comply with them. And marriages were zealously investigated by the police to ensure that they were not simply marriages of convenience – to the level, practically, of spying on the newly-weds.

Deportations too had been, and continued to be, on the increase. In 1977 they totalled 54,000. After that, the government stopped counting – or at least publishing the numbers. As with so much of Belgian law and administrative practice over this issue, the true situation remains hidden under layers of secretive bureaucracy; every so often ministerial edicts emerge, unremarked and undebated, tightening a screw here, closing an imaginary loophole there. Thus, doubtless many thousands of deportations have taken place, under the rubric of 'public security', 'no means of maintenance', etc., but only the occasional, most shocking case hits the headlines. One such incident involved shuttling several hundred gypsies – who were, at one stage, held for several days in a roadside car park – between Belgium and the Netherlands. And the introduction of compulsory visas for Turks and Moroccans has also led to an increase in expulsions.

The policing of control

The above is a history, similar in outline, to that of many European countries: the complexities of the law recall the German situation, the attitude to 'integration' is partly reminiscent of the French. There are, however, two aspects of Belgian racism that mark it out more specifically. One is the extent of internal, bureaucratic control over every facet of a 'foreign' worker's experience and day-to-day living; the other is the way it is policed.

In a country which, by its very nature, cannot be sealed completely at the border, immigration controls have effectively become internalised in every part of officialdom. This, combined with the largely unquestioned assumption of Belgian racial superiority, means that the institutionalisation of racism has reached unprecedented levels in Belgian society. So, on every 'foreigner', there is a file documenting periods of work and periods of unemployment, police reports, court reports, personal information on his/her family and, if a student, on the course of studies. And the file will follow the 'foreigner' everywhere. All foreigners have to register with a borough which, as of 1985, can refuse them permission to settle there. All sorts of documentation are needed for every official purpose, and more and more 'foreigners' are finding it difficult to obtain what they are entitled to. For every document or stamp of an administrative nature, they may have to wait for a lengthy period, or pay excessively – whether for a marriage permit, for members of their family to join them, for nationality purposes, for social or welfare benefits. A young 'foreigner' in Liège, for example, though born in Belgium, will, like his father before him, have to register his fingerprints with the police. And the police will check that the marriage a 'foreigner' has made is not a marriage of convenience.[7]

For, linking it all, linking the racism of the street with the racism of the local administration, with the racism of the government, with the racism of border control, is the police.

They are all-pervasive; they 'escort' the unwilling deportee to the transit centre, on to the aircraft. In 1980, a would-be Zairean refugee, Joseph Nsele, attempted to enter the country. He was refused, sent to Denmark and put on a flight back to Kinshasa. Attempting to enter Belgium again he was kept, forty days and forty nights, without money or passport, in the transit area (which is not regarded as Belgian territory and is, therefore, no one's responsibility). Dragged off by police and immigration officials for another flight to Zaire, beaten up, threatened with a gun, he was only saved by the intervention of the (American) pilot, who refused to carry him. He was finally granted refugee status after the saleswomen at the duty-free shop contacted Amnesty International.[8] Less fortunate was another Zairean refugee who, in 1987, was discovered to have been killed in the no-man's land of the transit centre.[9] Or there was the Moroccan deportee who, in 1982, was beaten up before his departure, tied to his seat, gagged – and found dead on arrival. Such brutal methods of deportation, with people 'hunted' for by the gendarmerie, caught in raids and manhandled into aircraft bound and handcuffed, are not uncommon.

Another young man, Joseph Silini, a Tunisian, was simply taken away by police after an identity check, beaten up and left for dead. He is now permanently disabled.[10] Such measures were, police explained, fairly common practice, necessary to 'calm' those so detained. Police raids on foreign workers' cafés, meeting places, etc., are commonplace – and are sometimes organised in almost para-military style, as on a number of cafés in Schaerbeek in 1981. Where there are larger communities of 'foreigners' – in certain districts of Brussels, for example – special squads are set up, the *'brigades canines'*. Their purpose, described as 'preventive', is, in fact, to intimidate. They are always there, always on the look-out, always on patrol, wherever migrant workers might be or might gather, to carry out identity checks, search for drugs – a menacing reminder of the state's power and the 'foreigner's' vulnerability.

The equation of 'foreigner' with 'criminal' made by politicians and the police, and endorsed by popular opinion, is carried on through the courts and in the prisons, where vastly disproportionate numbers of 'foreigners' find themselves. And, there is a double jeopardy for young people who, though they may have been born in Belgium, are still legally 'foreigners'. For, if convicted of serious crime (currently interpreted by the Ministry of Justice as anything meriting a one year sentence or longer), they are, like other foreigners, candidates for deportation, to a country they may never have seen, whose language they may scarcely even speak. This is in addition to serving a strict prison sentence. Moreover, in practice harsher and more punitive prison sentences are imposed on young 'foreigners' than is the case for their white Belgian counterparts convicted of similar offences. There is nothing, despite protests from human rights organisations, to prevent such young people serving both the prison sentence and the expulsion.* Since the 'one-year rule' for deportation (in the interests, naturally, of public security) was introduced in 1982, some 4,500 migrants have been deported in this way.

The rise of racism in the 1980s

If, despite the increasingly restrictive climate of the 1970s, there was still some measure of debate about rights for foreign workers; if political parties could talk of giving 'foreigners' the vote, during the 1980s this has all but disappeared. 'Foreigners' still have no political rights whatsoever, they are still effectively subject to expulsion on all kinds of grounds. An era of rising unemployment – the decline in the older, traditional, heavy industries, the shift in the nature of employment itself caused by the technological revolution, with the corresponding movement from full-time to part-time work (the so-called

---

* Since the European Commission of Human Rights ruled in October 1989 that such a procedure violates the right to family life guaranteed under the Human Rights Convention, the authorities have been reluctant to issue deportation orders if an individual was born in Belgium, or lived there from early childhood. However, there is a case which, at the time of writing, has just reached the Court of Human Rights, concerning a young Moroccan, who had lived in Belgium from the age of 7 months, and had been deported in 1984 after a long string of petty offences.[11]

flexible workforce) – has meant an increase in poverty and economic insecurity. Cuts in social and welfare benefits have increased the pressure. And the revival of inter-communal (Fleming/Walloon) conflict in the early 1980s, while contained by the creation of a more elaborate structure of government, has also served to render government even more remote and distrusted. Nor have the traditional institutions of the Left and the labour movement offered any clear direction, even as their constituencies have dwindled around them.

In this climate, the parties of the Right, the parties of racism and aggressive nationalism, have grown stronger, and so has the popular racism off which they feed, making the situation of 'foreigners' even more precarious.

At every stage, the government has simply responded by carrying out ever more repressive measures against foreign workers. They are held responsible for unemployment. '50,000 unemployed, so why foreign labour' is a fairly typical headline. In 1985, long-term unemployed foreign workers were offered 'repatriation' money by the government. The numbers involved may have been small, but the scapegoating implied was powerful, and served to cement popular prejudice. In 1984, further limits were put on family reunification. And, despite the anti-racist laws, certain boroughs were allowed to refuse rights of residence to 'foreigners'. The right of such refusal was necessary, argued the mayors of a number of boroughs in Brussels, 'as soon as the number of migrants exceeds a certain density which endangers national and public security, the maintenance of public order, the prevention of crime, the protection of health and morality, and the rights and freedoms of others'[12] – proof, if any were needed, of the danger that 'foreigners' posed to Belgian society. A whole segregation has grown up in housing and education, consigning 'foreigners' to the poorest and the worst.

Hysteria has been whipped up over would-be asylum-seekers: police raids and searches, identity and paper checks have become ever more commonplace, ever more zealous, ever more violent. In 1987, the law on refugees was changed fundamentally. Not only did it introduce a distinction between 'economic' and 'political' refugees, but it also abolished the automatic right of asylum-seekers to enter Belgian territory. Just as primary immigration was ended in 1974 – to 'protect our workers' – so the law on asylum was changed – to 'protect our poor'.

In 1987, the Minister of the Interior, expounding on the decline in the Belgian birthrate, declared that he dare not 'gamble on society in 2020'. He continued: 'We risk suffering the same fate as the Roman Empire when it was engulfed by the Barbarians. These are the Moroccans, the Turks, the Yugoslavs, the Muslims . . . They have nothing in common with our civilisation.'[13] Increasingly, in recent times, a stance against Islam and Islamic fundamentalism has been a threadbare cover for racist hostility to Muslims themselves.

In 1986, for example, about 100 heavily armed police, using water-cannon and armoured vehicles, were involved in closing down an Iranian cultural centre in Brussels – on the grounds of 'fears of an expansion of Islamic fundamentalism among the Muslim popu- lation.'[14] And the authorities in Schaerbeek have published and distributed brochures for students in which North Africans were described as terrorists and religious fundamentalists linked to drug- dealing.[15] More recently, when Arab local radio stations had the temerity to criticise western intervention in the Gulf, they were immediately threatened with closure.

Meanwhile, the Socialist Party has, apparently, come to the realisation that insufficient attention has been paid to the genuine fears of the Belgian working class over migration; that immigration controls should be stricter, and that 'foreigners' should not, after all, have the vote, either locally or nationally. Only the dismantling of the ghettos, and the dispersal of 'foreigners', according to the dictates of the 'threshold of tolerance' theory, would provide the conditions for 'integration'. 'Integration' is much touted by all parties, when at- tempting to put forth their most positive, thoughtful and 'caring' aspect. A vague and woolly idea at the best of times, it seems on all sides to amount to Belgian society doing little to accommodate itself to the 'foreigners' (except possibly, *possibly*, allowing the vote to the third generation*), while the 'foreigners' turn themselves into what? Cultural clones of the Vlaams Blok?

For this culture, which sees itself as the only route to civilisation, barely conceals a profound barbarity, expressed politically by the growing strength of parties such as Vlaams Blok or Forces Nouvelles and the Front National, expressed on the streets by brutal racist attacks. Under-age skinheads murdered a Burundese refugee in Louvain in September 1987; the same month a group of young Moroccan Christians were attacked by 'skinheads' wielding knives, chains and broken bottles in Overijse and a young girl (12 years old) was beaten up while waiting for a bus in Schaerbeek.[16] And in a suburb of Brussels, in October 1985, members of the far-right Forces Nouvelles attacked the home of a Moroccan family armed with steel bars, axes and knives.[17]

There is, it is true, a growing movement to protect and defend asylum-seekers; there is a movement against racism in the schools.

---

* This was one of the proposals made by a Royal Commission on Integration set up by the government in 1989. It also called for a stand against racism, and rejection of a repatriation policy. Reactions to it have been lukewarm, however, and none of its recommendations have so far been put into effect.

The deportations of Belgian-born 'foreigners' have been protested. Indeed, the passage of the anti-racist law was only finally brought about by large anti-racist demonstrations. Nonetheless, the tide is flowing strongly the other way. The far-right Vlaams Blok, for example (which comes out of a long tradition of Flemish nationalist linkages with nazism and fascism), has gained much credibility in recent years. Drawing its strength from both younger, highly educated Flemish nationalists and older, working-class people from poorer (traditionally socialist) districts, and aided by a right-wing press, it achieved something of an electoral breakthrough in 1988.* It won more than 4 per cent of the vote in twelve towns in Flanders, and polled over 17 per cent in Antwerp (a percentage that increased in the European elections to over 21 per cent). Among its demands is the forced mass transfer of all non-EC people away from Belgium, on the grounds that integration is undesirable and impossible, and a mix of cultures is disastrous. It is a demand echoed, albeit in far more muted form, even by the Flemish Liberal Party.

And, meanwhile, on the streets and in the detention centres, in the ghettos and in the town halls, the police, the officials, the politicos, the youth, the citizens carry out, in a different strain, the type of crude, brute racism, spawned initially in the brute, crude colonialism of King Leopold's Congo.

References

1   F.E. Huggett, *Modern Belgium* (London, 1969).
2   *Europa World Yearbook* (London, 1990).
3   Ibid.
4   Much of the information in this section particularly, but also throughout, comes from A. Martens, *Diviser pour regner: racisme comme stratégie* (Antwerp, 1985).
5   Romsée, quoted in ibid.
6   Huggett, op. cit.
7   *Diviser pour regner*, op. cit.
8   Ibid.
9   Le Drapeau Rouge (16/17 and 29 January 1987).
10   *Diviser pour regner*, op. cit.
11   *Migration Newssheet* (October 1990).
12   Statement issued by mayors of Brussels, 1983.
13   *Magazine Exclusief* (September-November 1987).
14   *Le Drapeau Rouge* (13 February 1986).
15   *Solidaire* (11 June 1986) and *Le Soir* (12 September 1986).
16   *Solidaire* (No 39, 7 October 1987).
17   *Le Drapeau Rouge* (25 October 1985).

* The equivalents in the French-speaking areas, the Front National and Forces Nouvelles, have not had the same electoral impact as Vlaams Blok – partly because of the division within the Right itself, partly because, in Brussels particularly, the Socialist Party has more successfully presented itself as 'anti-foreigner'.

MARCO MARTINIELLO and PAUL KAZIM

Italy: two perspectives
Racism in paradise?*

The beginning of the 1970s marked a fundamental reversal in the history of migration in Italy. For more than a century before that, the transalpine peninsula had been one of the greatest suppliers of labour power, first to North America and Latin America, then to other European countries, especially France, and also to Australia. There are today more than five million Italians dispersed throughout the world. But Italian emigration started to diminish even as the economic 'miracle' began to take shape, exclusively in the north and centre of the 'boot'. Now, the only Italian emigrants are those who put their mental abilities at the service of world industry – to which one should add the likes of Berlusconi and Benedetti. Thus, while most European countries began to erect legal barriers at the beginning of the 1970s to prevent migration, Italy became, almost unawares, an importer of labour power, enticed by the image of paradise conjured up in the phrase 'made in Italy'. It is only recently, especially since 1986 and more spectacularly since the summer of 1989, that immigration has become an important issue in the media and in politics, in debates which cross the whole of Italian society.

Some characteristics of immigration in Italy

A preliminary remark – when one speaks of immigration and

Marco Martiniello is attached to the European Institute of Florence University, and the Catholic University of Louvain. *Paul Kazim* is a researcher with Moonlight Films, an independent, black production company, based in London.
*A French version of this first piece has appeared in *Hommes et Migrations* (November 1990).

Race & Class, 32(3), 1991

immigrants in Italy, one is not referring to the rich retired Germans or English who live in the Tuscan countryside, or to American students or businessmen based in Florence, Rome or Milan. The term 'immigrant' is only applied to non-EC citizens from a Third World country who come to Italy to work. As for refugees and candidates for political asylum, they constitute a separate sub-category – the *'immigrati extracommunitari'*.

How many of these immigrants are there? At the moment, no-one in Italy can say precisely, though everyone has his or her own estimate. There is a real war of numbers which is monopolising the energy of social science researchers. The National Institute of Statistics (ISTAT) recently estimated the non-EC presence in Italy as being 963,000 persons,[1] a figure which includes Americans, Swiss and Austrians. As far as Third World 'immigrants' alone are concerned, their numbers, according to the most serious estimates,[2] do not exceed 800,000 – that is, just over 1 per cent of the population. And yet some people talk of an 'invasion' to characterise the migratory phenomenon in Italy!

Certainly, the impression of an invasion is created by the greater visibility of a fraction of these immigrants who live in the centre of the large towns. So, for example, the area around the Termini railway station in Rome gives to commuters – but also to tourists – a false image of the real situation, simply because of the concentration of *extracommunitari* who are easily recognised by the colour of their skin. This form of appropriation of certain parts of the urban space, nevertheless, points to a characteristic of immigration in Italy. It is primarily an urban phenomenon. Thus, the capital, Milan, Turin, Bologna, Florence and Naples are often major poles of attraction for immigrants, who move readily from one of these towns to another. There is also a transitory movement to the countryside, rural regions calling for seasonal immigrant workers for various harvests.

The origins of immigrants now living in Italy correspond to two different phases of migration: the earlier, mainly covering the period from 1970 to 1985; the recent, which began after that date. The first consisted mainly of Africans from the Italian ex-colonies and Iranian political refugees, but also included Filipino domestic workers and, in some parts of Sicily, Moroccans and Tunisians. But after 1986, Senegalese, as well as new waves of Tunisians and Ghanaians, began to arrive. There are now a number of different nationalities, mostly African and Asian, among the non-European immigrant population in the peninsula. With the exception of women domestic workers from the Philippines and Cape Verde, however, most of the new immigrants are young men, already urbanised in their countries of origin and with relatively high educational levels: 36.5 per cent have secondary school certificates or a university diploma and 23.3 per cent a professional diploma, according to a survey carried out by ISPES in December 1989. It is, however, very unusual for them to find employment in Italy commensurate with their diplomas and qualifications. They are nearly all economically active, but their entry into the Italian labour market is almost always precarious and illegal.

Immigrants gain employment in Italy in two main ways. On the one hand, some are employed in areas which have been abandoned by Italians. In other words, by accepting employment on conditions which Italians refuse, immigrants supply an unsatisfied demand in a number of sectors. In agriculture, immigrant workers are used for the various harvests, in several regions in both the north and south. They receive derisory salaries, often have no work contract and, consequently, no legal protection. In industry, small- and medium-sized enterprises in the north are increasingly seeking foreign labour already in Italy, either legally or illegally, to undertake unskilled work for wages which Italians would refuse. Furthermore, immigrant workers are sometimes recruited legally, then submitted to a special regime of flexible working. This was the case, for example, in the 1989 agreement signed between the Turin employers and trade unions over the legal engagement of immigrant workers to replace Italian workers in night shifts, on Sundays or on bank holidays.[3] One should, therefore, treat with caution the theory about competition between Italians and foreigners on the labour market.

On the other hand, a second group seem to have created their own sphere where demand did not seem to exist before – as Say would have put it, the availability of immigrant labour seems to have created its own demand. In travelling sales, in particular, there is no explicit demand for immigrant labour, and yet this is often the point of entry into employment for many immigrants. And if one looks at the situation more closely, it appears that the more or less legal zones of the market economy which control such activities have rapidly created a demand for immigrant labour. In fact, immigrant travelling sales is largely controlled by illegal organisations which have taken maximum advantage of the most vulnerable section of immigrant labour. It is the same logic which leads organised crime to recruit immigrants into prostitution or soft drugs trafficking. Leaving part of the soft drugs trade in the hands of powerless immigrants allows its real controllers to increase profits while reducing risks.

It is clear that this type of exploitation of immigrants is only possible when there is a complete vacuum in immigration policy, which was the case until recently. In fact, most immigrants had no legal status or rights in Italian society until the adoption of the 'Martelli law', to which I shall return later. And obviously, people without protection need to deploy every means of survival, even if it is illegal.

From this brief outline of immigration certain aspects specific to Italy emerge:
– Unlike the immigration to northern Europe after the Second World War, that to Italy is not the result of explicit recruitment organised by the state and employers with trade union endorsement. It is, rather, the result of a conjuncture between an implicit appeal from Italy and 'push' factors in the countries of origin.
– Italy is still mainly at the stage of the immigration of workers, even if family reunification is already taking place for those who came in on the earlier waves of immigration.
– Immigration in Italian society is relatively modest in quantitative terms compared to the older European countries of immigration.

Italy's response to immigration

As a new phenomenon, immigration poses questions and difficulties for society in general, as well as for politicians, since Italy is much more accustomed to exporting its poor than receiving them from other countries.

As far as society in general is concerned, immigration has delivered indirectly a strong upper-cut to the image of *'Italiani, brava gente'* (Italians – a kind people) that Italians love to present and which is recognised by the world up to a certain point. After a long period of public and also political indifference to immigration and immigrants, Italian society has started to show increasing signs of unease and intolerance towards immigrants. Verbal as well as physical attacks on the 'new Italians' have become more and more frequent since the mid-1980s. Two of the most serious – and which were most discussed – were the assassination of a young black South African exile in the Naples region in August 1989 and the anti-immigrant raid during the Florence carnival in March 1990, which reached the French and British press. These two events, far from isolated, stoked up the debate on racism in Italy significantly. Italian society has come to question itself about the possibility of its own hidden racism. For some, there is no doubt that Italy is racist, just like other European countries. For others, it is not a question of racism but of the problems which arise from an inadequate sharing out of the insufficient resources produced by the Italian 'miracle'. Still others see Italy as going through a pre-racist period which, if we are not careful, could lead to racist wars in Italian cities.

Italian society today is going through a profound identity crisis as a result of the erosion of the two traditional poles of its social structure, one centred in the Catholic church and the other in the Communist party. Above and beyond the crisis of their reproduction and ideological renewal is the fact that these two groups of institutions, so central to Italian society, can no longer fulfil the functions of socialisation and identification for the younger generation as once they used to do. In a country like Italy, where the national entity is of recent origin, and somewhat fragile, the decline of the traditional poles of social identification could be the origin of a sense of insecurity and a diffuse malaise in society.

The growing economic dualism of Italian society is also bringing similar consequences. The wound, which has never healed, of modern Italian history – the economic backwardness of the southern regions of the 'boot' – seems to be getting worse. While the northern regions are at the forefront of technological progress, enjoy exceptionally high levels of productivity and are thus among the foremost areas of advanced capitalism, the south, with some exceptions, is stagnating. Unemployment there is very high, productivity weak, technological development slow. This unequal development, and the interpretations which are given of it, deepen the malaise to which I have already referred.

This malaise expresses itself most directly in two phenomena, which are also connected to displays of intolerance towards non-European immigrants and towards southerners. First, there is the violence around football, which is the action of organised groups of pseudo-supporters who target not just supporters of the opposite team but also immigrant workers. Thus, the aggressors at the 'Mardi Gras' festival in Florence belonged to the 'ultras' of Fiorentina. Or again, last May, Juventas supporters who had to change trains at Genoa on their way back from a match in the south, attacked several North Africans who were in their way. And that is not counting the anti-southern and anti-immigrant chants which one hears more and more in Italian stadiums. Second, there is the growing phenomenon of 'leagues' (Lega Lombarda, Liga Veneta, etc.); right-wing regional parties of the north whose success depends on mobilising anti-southern and anti-immigrant sentiments.

Thus, immigration and racism constitute major political issues, both domestically and on the European level in the run-up to 1992. Internally, electoral considerations seem to guide the positions taken and the proposals made by the different parties about immigration and, more precisely, migration policy. At the European level, Italy is attempting to get rid of the image prevalent in other EC countries, of having 'leaky frontiers', which are considered to pose serious difficulties over free movement of European nationals within the EC after 1992. Following direct or indirect, implicit or explicit pressure from the rest of the Community, it has set up mechanisms to control immigrants: to stop them, on the one hand, and, on the other, to 'integrate' those*

---

* The concept of 'integration' poses the same sort of confusions in Italy as elsewhere.

who are already within its borders. Hence, the 'Martelli law' of 28 February 1990, which also deals with political refugees. This law (named after the vice-president of the Council), together with law 943 passed in December 1986, constitutes the framework of Italian migration policy. The basis of the 'Martelli law' was a government decree adopted in December 1989 aimed at solving the urgent problems of immigration. To control migration, it posits an annual programme for the entry of immigrant workers to be established jointly by the ministries concerned (foreign affairs, interior, planning and employment). It is important to stress that in an interview given to the daily *La Repubblica* on 9 June 1990, Martelli clearly implied that, from 1991, frontiers would be virtually closed. As for 'integration', the law confirms the regularisation of foreigners living in Italy before December 1989, which had already been promised by the government. As from 29 June 1990, it is impossible for illegal immigrants to gain access to legal status. Thus, Italy is attempting to pass as rapidly as possible from having no legal conditions on immigration to aligning itself with other EC countries so as to make a unified Community policy on migration possible. In a way, Italy has to jump a number of stages and simply follow, as closely as possible, the pattern set by other European countries. This desire to line up alongside its EC partners shows itself particularly in Italy's signing of the Schengen agreements in October 1990.

MARCO MARTINIELLO

Racism is no paradise!

To nearly 200 Bangladeshi, Indian, Pakistani and Sri Lankan immigrant workers on hunger strike in Milan, the giant hoarding suspended high opposite the city's famous Duomo cathedral, advertising the 'True Colours of Benetton', was nothing but a cruel joke. Gazing down, in an image of racial harmony, were two women, one black, one white, holding a Chinese baby. But these immigrant workers had already seen the true colours of Italian society.

Miserable, cold and hungry, they sat on cardboard sheets in a make-shift camp on Milan's Piazza Vetra, a large, grassy, crapping zone for many of the city's dogs. Highly qualified, they had come to Italy, equipped with degrees, doctorates and high hopes. But wakened to their Italian reality, they organised themselves as the Milan branch of the United Asian Workers' Association, a body set up by homeless Asian workers in Rome. Step two was to embark on a desperate hunger strike – not something they had anticipated writing home about to their families.

'We thought Italy was a civilised country where we could find jobs, good money and nice homes. But they treat dogs better than us. We were so wrong', said Mohammed Riaz. It was an understandable mistake: Milan, seen by these men from Dacca, Lahore and Delhi, was Europe's citadel of a designer capitalism that promised them jobs, money and homes.

Riaz and his colleagues resorted to the hunger strike after being unceremoniously removed from their sit-in under the Largo Treves offices of Milan's social security chief, Roberto Bernardelli. He had promised them 300 blankets. Consistent with his past promises of accommodation for these immigrants, promises as vacant as many of Milan's buildings, Bernardelli's blankets never materialised. As the hunger strike began, Bernardelli, the Italian flag hanging behind him, gave interviews about the gradual but inevitable acceptance by Italian society of its new multi-racial reality.

There was, though, nothing gradual about the need of these workers for accommodation. Collectively huddled in nearby cloisters for warmth and security, the hunger strikers were forcibly cleared out by police in a drenching downpour. The hunger strike was over, but they were still living on Milan's streets. An occupation of the Santa Ambrogio church ended when police threw them back on to the streets. The hunger strikers had earlier been removed from an empty council building – on the premise that it was unfit for human habitation. Others were thrown out of a disused garage and moved to a fairground.

Arriving in Milan from Rome, they had encountered a city where unemployment is low but jobs are few. A brusque, unfriendly city where African migrants wander the streets, trying to sell leather goods and cigarettes to style-conscious Milanese, who would rather spend extravagantly on Gucci and Vacheron-Constantin designer items than buy no-style, no-label goods from a nobody African hawker.

They thought Milan must have more to offer than Rome. Italy's capital had dashed many of their hopes, offering them no work, and only hotel accommodation that quickly ate into whatever money they had brought with them. Time was passed sitting amongst the trees of the Piazza del Cinquecento or on the steps of the Piazza della Repubblica. They watched young Senegalese men laying down their blanket displays of bags, wallets, purses, cigarettes, leather straps, leather belts, sunglasses and beads, items they forlornly hoped to sell to tourists.

Near Rome's main bus terminal, they saw large groups of Filipino men and women chatting, playing cards, eating rice and chicken out of large 'cook-up' pots, as they waited to go on their night or early shifts as cleaners, au-pairs, hotel porters and kitchen staff. In Rome, only the Filipinos have any sort of job or security.

Two months or so later, tired and broke, many of those who would end up on hunger strike made their way to Rome's Stazione Centrale where they saw Somalian men and women sitting, talking at tables in the concourse cafe, much to the irritation of the Roman waiters urging them to order or move on. But the hunger strikers were most interested in checking train fares and times to the north – to Turin, Genoa, Bologna, Reggio Nell'Emilia, Florence and, of course, Milan, the 'real Italy', where they expected jobs and homes.

Italy's post-war economic growth has rested on such a migration of workers from the underdeveloped rural south to the rapaciously industrialising urban north. But Milan's economy did not need this latest set of arrivals from the south. Most of these immigrants had been in Italy since March 1989, drawn by the Martelli decree, the amnesty granted to illegal immigrants. Mistakenly, they believed the amnesty meant that socialist Italy at least would welcome them with open arms. Then, too late, they understood the true nature of the amnesty tactic – a political expedient intended to 'regularise' and take out the illegal work-force from the labour market, while at the same time stopping the entry of further 'illegals'.

The Martelli law of 28 February 1990 outlawed new Third World immigration by imposing visa requirements on people entering Italy from Morocco, Tunisia, Algeria, Turkey, Mauritania and Senegal. It provided a semblance of security for Italy's unauthorised immigrant workers – provided they beat the 28 June 1990 deadline, such workers were told they could obtain a residence permit.

Technically, a residence permit guarantees an employment card. But for those immigrant workers at the Piazza Vetra who did have low-paid, cash-only jobs as brick-layers and drivers, legality made them less attractive and more expensive to their employers. Better to be illegal and earning than be authorised and starving was how they viewed the amnesty.

Thus, to the immigrants the amnesty was scarcely worth the paper on which it was written. 'I wrote it with great sadness. The amnesty has a general principle that's very severe', Martelli said.[4] Genuinely saddened or not, Martelli helped buy time for the government and his ruling Socialist party. The Lega Lombarda, an extreme right-wing group advocating separatism for the rich Lombardy region that includes Milan, was fanning popular resentment against immigrants. The amnesty would buy time for the government – but the Lega's call for a referendum helped it to enlarge its 20 per cent vote-catching power. Already, the Lega Lombarda had successfully whipped up local resentment against the presence of 600 homeless and mainly jobless Moroccan men, women and children at La Cascina Rosa, a shanty town erected on a derelict farm, located in a prosperous high-rise inner suburb of Milan. The Carabinieri, acting on the orders of the local magistrate, dragged the peacefully protesting Moroccans from the one haven they had from attack at night. Just weeks before, 26-year-old Foaud Ouchbani had been brutally murdered in central Milan, hit over the head by a bottle as he tried to sell cigarettes.

La Cascina Rosa, its makeshift mosque, barber's shop, surgery and restaurant, its electricity supply routed by cables from nearby street lamps, was razed to the ground by the Carabinieri. The local magistrate justified the raid on grounds that La Cascina Rosa was insanitary. True, there was a cesspool, but more smelly was the Left politics that decreed that the only way to stop the electoral advance of the extreme Right was to destroy the self-made community of a deprived underclass.

Sending in the Carabinieri was a short-term, clumsy political expedient for Milan city council. Bernardelli's office wanted to appear to the Milanese as tough on the immigrant, and then humanitarian after the kick-in. The fear was that the Milanese were beginning to pay too much heed to the solutions offered by the extreme Right. Across Italy, unauthorised workers like these were solving employers' cheap labour problems. In Milan, where the need for cheap labour was almost zero, they were a convenient political scapegoat. Indulging anti-immigrant sentiment was seen as the only way to stop the extreme Right.

After the 'amnesty', other EC governments could no longer deride Italy as the easy way into Fortress Europe for Third World immigrants. Italy could now set up its stall in Schengenland,* the unofficial title for the no-passport zone between France, Germany, the Netherlands, Belgium and Luxembourg. Once Italy had been refused entry into Schengen on account of it being Europe's weak immigration link. Now Italy has built its section of the Euro iron curtain.

Proof that the amnesty had failed to provide any real security for Italy's illegal immigrants came in a series of incidents last autumn, three months after the amnesty deadline. Italian youths set fire to an immigrant hostel in Bolzano, near Bologna. Some 120 homeless North African immigrants questioned whether the arson had been legitimated by Bolzano town councillors in their banning of any more black people from settling there.

Turin and Verona, two of the most industrial northern cities, banned immigrants from washing car windscreens at traffic lights. (From Palermo in Sicily to Naples and Milan this work has often been the only source of income for many immigrants.) African fruit-pickers were attacked in the vineyards, orange groves and orchards around Naples. In the same area, along darkened roads, illuminated only by the eery fires lit by prostitutes advertising their services, African

* On the Schengen agreement, see the article by Tony Bunyan in this issue.

women were attacked by pimps and prostitutes angered at being under-cut by 'exotic' competition.

Italy is now a society worried by the implications of its increasing dependency on cheap, illegal foreign labour. But, to keep it cheap, it must be illegal. And to keep Italy's economy fully powered, this form of Third World development aid must succeed in getting into the country; the politics of the amnesty must remain a charade.

In a country where tomatoes are almost sacred, the Italian press reported that unauthorised African migrants in the Apulia and Puglia regions picked almost 50 per cent of the country's tomato harvest. Tomato prices, it was reported, were kept low by employing illegal African labourers at low rates of pay with no contracts.

Migrants had arrived in Italy throughout 1990 by boat via Tunis, coming to the Sicilian ports of Palermo, Trapani, Catania and Mazara del Vallo. Most were able to enter on tourist visas, even though immigration officers knew they were not tourists but potential settlers hoping to stay. Those put back on the returning ferries had been removed from Italy before, their glued passport pages slit open to reveal the removal stamps.

Yet potential immigrants were still entering Italy by clandestine and more dangerous means. Fishing boats from Tunis carried many immigrants to the southern Sicilian port of Mazara del Vallo, the closest Italian town to Tunisia, to Africa. Sleepy, blazing hot Mazara became the centre of national concern when it was revealed that almost 11 per cent of its population were non-Italian, non-EC nationals. Though more akin to Bognor Regis, Italian society came to see slumbering Mazara as Italy's Marseilles, where Europe not only meets but is swamped by Africa.

Nearly 50 per cent of Mazara's fishing boats employ cheap Tunisian or Moroccan crews. It is one of many statistics that now haunts Italian society. The biggest bogey is the projection that Italy's population will fall from its current 56 million to 45 million in 2045, of whom only one in four will be active workers. Italy, notwithstanding the Pope, has the lowest birthrate in Europe and is already paying for 19 million pensions.

Cheap Third World labour will become an even greater necessity unless Italians can heed the advice of their Labour Minister Carlo Donat Cattin who called on Italians to produce more babies 'to keep away armadas of immigrants from the southern shores of the Mediterranean'. It was a call that was echoed by Umberto Eco: 'We are not facing an immigration phenomenon. We are facing a migratory phenomenon. And like all great migrations, its final result will be an inexorable change in habits, and unstoppable interbreeding that changes the colour of skin, hair and eyes.'[5]

But Catholic Italians are becoming more like their European

Protestant counterparts: they want less children and more material gain. Nor do they want the dirty and tedious jobs in the hospitals, the fields or the domestic jobs – they want Third World workers to slop out Italian society. But the fear is growing that the Italian nation will be slopped out in the process. Either way, Third World migrant workers will face further angry and violent resentment for being, in reality, Italy's economic saviours.

PAUL KAZIM

References

1   The ISTAT estimates are for 30 April 1990, and were published in May 1990.
2   See the work of Enrico Pugilese, especially his article in *Il Manifesto* (17 May 1990), p.10.
3   *Il Manifesto* (7 October 1989), p.12.
4   Interview with BBC2 Newsnight, 18 May 1990.
5   Interview in *L'Espresso* (July 1990).

Variants

Spain: racism at the frontier

The abolition of national frontiers in 1992 has probably more political and historical significance for Spain than for any other country in Europe. Ever since the premature decline of the Spanish empire, the country – which once dominated Europe and played such a major role in establishing European hegemony on a world scale – has been something of a political and economic anachronism on the continent. For the ruling socialist party, the PSOE, the year of Spain's formal entry into the EEC marks an essential step towards the modernisation of the country and the creation of a social-democratic utopia south of the Pyrenees. 1992 is also a significant date in Spanish history for other reasons. In 1492, Christopher Columbus 'discovered' Latin America for the benefit of Spanish imperialism and, shortly afterwards, the rulers of the newly unified kingdom ordered one of the first mass deportations of a population on racial grounds in history – the expulsion of the Jews. The same combination of xenophobia, religious fanaticism and greed resulted in the subsequent expulsion of the Arabs and the virtual annihilation of the indigenous civilisations of Latin America. In spite of sharing the same historical link between racism and imperialist expansion common to other European countries, however, racism never assumed the kind of political importance in modern Spain that it has in other former imperialist powers. The racial dimension was never a very significant ideological component of Spanish fascism, for example, and the 'national-catholicism' of Franco probably owed more to the inquisition than it did to nazism.

Not only did racist political creeds fail to have any national impact in twentieth-century Spain but, until recently, the Spanish were the subject of considerable racist stereotyping from their more advanced neighbours in the north. During the 1960s, more than a million Spanish workers from poorer regions of the country went abroad to work – for the booming industrial economies of Germany, Switzerland and Belgium, in particular. More often than not, these Iberian migrant workers found themselves exposed to the same kind of discrimination accorded to their present-day counterparts from the Third World. 'A large number of bars in Brussels', wrote a young Spanish lawyer called Felipe Gonzalez, who was studying temporarily in Belgium at the time, 'had an announcement: no entry for Spaniards, Africans and North Africans . . . the railway stations are packed with Spaniards who spend hour upon hour in a state of disorientation. They're not shown the slightest consideration and are in the saddest human and spiritual misery.' The attitudes of many northern Europeans towards their southern neighbour were summed up in the well-known truism that 'Africa begins at the Pyrenees', and the Spanish were attributed with all the 'typical' Mediterranean vices of sloth, corruption, violence and cultural backwardness. In turn, these same characteristics were, and still are, projected on to the inhabitants of the underdeveloped south within Spain itself – in particular, the country's large gypsy population, which has been marginalised and discriminated against for centuries, while, at the same time, its culture has been appropriated into the national Spanish heritage.

Today, the scenes which once distressed the future leader of the PSOE in Belgium can be seen all over Spain itself, and racism, at both an official and a popular level, has become an increasingly common feature of national life. The problem is a relatively recent one. Spain never experienced the high levels of immigration from its former colonies that took place in Britain or France. Nor was there any organised importation of foreign labour into the country carried out by Spanish companies or the state. Instead, immigration has been largely sporadic and uneven. Nevertheless, the immigrant population has grown steadily in recent years, and there are now approximately 800,000 non-European immigrants living in the country.

Rigid immigration controls have ensured that nearly 300,000 of the immigrant population are living and working illegally. Of these, the majority are Latin Americans, followed by North Africans, Filipinos, Portuguese, Guineans and Central Africans. The majority of non-white immigrants in Spain work in industry and agriculture, doing the kind of jobs that Spanish workers no longer want to do. They can be found in the mines of Asturias, in the textile factories of Catalonia, in the flower-growing fields of the Costa Brava and the big export farms of Almeria and Andalucia. Others work as day labourers on construction sites or drift into the underground economy, selling junk souvenirs and cheap sunglasses in resort towns along the coast. Most Filipino and African women work as maids or domestic servants in the big cities of Madrid or Barcelona. The importation of Filipino maids into Spain has become a highly profitable enterprise in some quarters. Many are attracted to Spain by shady companies who promise them the chance to study and find a good job when they arrive. Instead, they find themselves stranded without money or work permits, with no option other than to accept the jobs for which they were recruited unwittingly, receiving as little as 50,000 pesetas (£200) a month for working twelve hours a day.

Other immigrants enter Spain through the Canary Islands with the intention of entering France, and end up staying in Spain only when they are unable to cross the frontier. They pick up what work they can find through the immigrant grapevine, living in cheap *pensions* and shopfronts or work huts and dormitory accommodation provided by their employers. Long hours, low wages, poor working and living conditions and the lack of any job security are the chief characteristics of Spain's new immigrant underclass. A dense thicket of bureaucratic legislation makes legal status impossible, thus reinforcing their economic marginalisation. Even the act of applying for legalisation may cost a migrant worker his or her job, since reluctant employers would then have to register them with social security. Without legal status, binding contracts with employers are impossible to achieve and migrant workers have little or no union protection. Instead, they are forced to live a marginalised existence on the fringes of Spanish society under the constant threat of being sacked or deported.

Socially, the situation of most immigrants is little better. Unlike Latin American immigrants, whose shared language and cultural background makes assimilation relatively easy, the majority of migrant workers form a despised and ghettoised sub-group within the communities in which they live. In some cases, immigrant workers are deliberately kept separate from the surrounding population by their employers, in order to avoid unwelcome attention from the authorities. In other cases, the process of social isolation is achieved through the established mechanisms of popular racism. Just as Spanish workers once found themselves prevented from entering bars in the 'civilised' north, so many black and Arab immigrants have received similar treatment in Spain. On Sunday afternoons it is a common sight to see small groups of black and Arab workers gathered together in railway stations and public places, with no money to spend or anywhere to go, ostracised at all levels from the surrounding community.

In recent years, the disturbing rise in racist violence in many parts of the country has resulted in more brutal manifestations of local hostility. On 20 May 1989, a Guinean worker had his hands broken in a bar in Almeria where he had gone to have a drink after work. In Tarragona, an illegal Moroccan construction worker was beaten to death by two Spaniards in a drunken fight. And in a small town in Catalonia, a national scandal was created when the local mayor tried, unsuccessfully, to enforce an identity card system for black workers in the town. In various parts of the country, there has been an alarming increase in acts of physical violence and harassment directed at the immigrant population, ranging from near lynchings to car-burnings and attacks in the street. The violence has not yet reached the levels of France or England, but it has become serious enough, so that even the socialist foreign minister Fernando Ordonez was forced to admit that 'Spain is experiencing a dangerous racist escalation'.

That such statements have not been matched by any official action is hardly surprising, considering that the legislation introduced by the PSOE is, in large part, responsible for the continued exploitation and marginalisation of Spain's non-white immigrants in the first place. The cornerstone of state racism is the notorious Ley de la Estranjera, or foreigners law. This iniquitous piece of legislation was introduced in 1985 specifically to curb the flow of immigrants from the African continent into Spain. The introduction of what many consider to be the toughest immigration law in Europe was partly the result of EC pressure on the Spanish government to close what is, in effect, Europe's geographical frontier with Africa and the first port of call for many immigrants seeking access to the rest of the continent. Last year, the Spanish Association for Human Rights declared in its annual report that the PSOE had 'taken on uncritically and in a resolute manner the repressive policy of the European Community towards non-EEC nationals'. And recently, a French government official warned that Spain would jeopardise friendly relations between the two countries if it did not do more to prevent the entry of illegal immigrants into France.

Certainly, the PSOE cannot be accused of shirking its responsibilities. Since the introduction of the Ley de la Estranjera, the number of arrests of illegal immigrants has tripled and the number of deportations has risen from 975 in 1985 to 4,739 in 1989. In addition, there has been a sharp increase in the refusal of right of asylum and, in 1989, 35,612 people were denied entrance at the frontier. The Ley de la Estranjera has provided the police with the legal means to harass the black and Arab immigrant population indiscriminately, with street searches and police raids becoming increasingly common. On occasions, where the Ley de la Estranjera has not provided sufficient justification for expulsions, the authorities have deported people simply for being 'undesirables'. In Catalonia, the proximity of the Olympic Games has provoked a crackdown on illegal immigrants and drugdealers, both of whom are usually regarded as the same thing by the authorities. In May 1990, a massive police raid on the towns of Vic and Osona resulted in the arrests of seventy Moroccan workers, fifty of whom were deported. In the wake of the deportations, hundreds of illegal workers went into hiding all over Catalonia, many of them fleeing into the mountains to avoid arrest.

The brutal manner in which the arrests were carried out and the fact that many of the deportees had been living in Spain for years drew sustained criticism from trade unions, church groups and human rights organisations. To its credit, the Spanish press was almost universal in its criticism of the Ley de la Estranjera and a series of articles drew public attention to the plight of the immigrant communities in Spain. 'It appears', said one journalist from the conservative daily *La Vanguardia*, 'that the Ley de la Estranjera was the logical conclusion and the colophon of the expulsion of the Jews 500 years ago.'

Neither the Catalan nor the national government showed any great remorse for the deportations, however, and the PSOE remains as cheapest, unskilled labour where required – and to do all this under the guise of humanitarianism. Increasingly, what gets relegated are the social and humanitarian considerations.

It is not often recognised that Switzerland itself was once, during the first half of the nineteenth century, a country of emigration. 'Mother dear, give me a 100 lire, I want to go to America', is a song still sung by children today. But, with large-scale industrialisation from the mid-nineteenth century onwards, came a complete reversal. By 1914, foreign immigrants totalled about 15 per cent of the population, about the same proportion as today.

Switzerland's reputation as a haven for refugees stemmed originally from its liberal, federal constitution of 1848, promulgated at a time of massive social and political change throughout Europe. Refugees began to flee to Switzerland from their own repressive, monarchical states, pointing to the violence, injustice and social misery of their homelands. So well-known was Switzerland as a haven for dissidents that, in 1890, Bismarck, chancellor of the newly formed German nation, infiltrated informers on them into Switzerland and, by exerting diplomatic pressure on the Swiss government, succeeded in having a special prosecutor appointed charged with surveillance of alien inhabitants – a practice that was to continue, though in different forms, in later years.

Switzerland's basically liberal policies were, however, to undergo a change, with the constitution itself being amended in 1925 after a heated campaign against foreign infiltration. Immigration had already been drastically reduced during and after the First World War, and stayed low during the subsequent period of economic crisis. But, with the rise of fascism prior to the Second World War, came a new wave of asylum-seekers, especially Jewish refugees, whom nonetheless the government attempted to ward off. Racism and anti-Semitism were stirred up by Swiss fascist groups, like the National Front, which put pressure on government and established political parties to halt the flow. So that, for example, until almost the end of the war, refugees fleeing for 'racial reasons' (that is Jews) could not be classed as 'political asylum-seekers'. And the Swiss authorities collaborated with the German in 1938 over marking the passports of German Jews with a special stamp – illustrative of the tendency within Swiss policy of curtailing, even closing off, admission to asylum-seekers as soon as world events threw them up in large numbers.

A certain liberalisation of policy, coinciding with a period of greater economic prosperity, followed the Second World War, with refugees coming mainly from Communist countries. At the same time, increasing numbers of foreign workers (mainly from Europe) were brought in to fuel the economic boom. But such liberalisation was short-lived. From the early 1960s, right-wing groups began to campaign around the issue of foreign immigration and, from 1963 onwards, quotas began to be set over how many foreign workers could be employed in an enterprise. From 1970, fixed quotas were set for the entry of those allowed in on one-year permits. Throughout this period, and subsequently, attempts were made by the racist Right to hold referenda among the whole population on the presence of migrants and foreigners in the country. Though none ultimately succeeded (some only failing by a very narrow margin), they have always commanded enough support, not only to torpedo any positive measures to improve the position of foreigners, but also to push government policy into making further concessions to the racists.

The current situation
By the end of 1989, Switzerland had, according to official statistics, an alien population of just over one million (1,040,325), which is 15.6 per cent of the Swiss population of 6.67 million. Of these, some have settlement permits, are free to change employment, can move from one canton to another and can have their residence permits extended without limit. 'Annual residents', on the other hand, have to have their residence and work permits renewed every year. After an uninterrupted stay of one year, their families may join them. According to 1987 figures, there are, in addition, 156,725 so-called seasonal workers, who are allowed to work and live in Switzerland for a maximum of nine months in any one year.

As the economy prospers, so the numbers of foreigners/aliens are allowed to increase – and so do complaints that the figure is getting too high. Conversely, after 1974, during a period of poor economic performance, the numbers of aliens decreased, from over 1,065,000 (in 1974) to around 900,000 in 1977. They began to rise again after 1980. This trend is even more pronounced in the case of the seasonal workers – with 194,000 in 1973, 61,000 in 1976, and rising dramatically again in the 1980s.

The seasonal workers are in a particularly weak position, absorbing directly the impact of economic change and fluctuation – as a sort of 'prosperity buffer'. They live in constant anxiety as to whether they will be recalled to work in the coming season, and have only the most limited rights to change their jobs. Working mostly within construction, catering and agriculture, the real function of such seasonal workers is to prevent labour shortages in firms that are not fully integrated into the labour market and which offer inferior conditions or low wages. Seasonal vacillations within the labour market are only a pretext. Furthermore, seasonal workers have no rights for their families to join them, and no right to unemployment benefit. And, because they are in such a vulnerable position, they are treated callously in cases of illness, accident etc.

Seasonal workers who manage to work for thirty-six months (their maximum allowance) within four consecutive years can qualify for an annual residence permit. This is easier said than done, for if there are any gaps in their periods of work, they have to start all over again from scratch. Few qualify – just over 12,500 in 1989.

Yet this provision, limited as it is, has recently come under fire, with employers demanding its abolition. Under the federal policy of stabilising foreign immigration, only limited numbers of aliens are allowed entry. But what employers most want at present are specialist skilled workers, and they are demanding precedence for these at the expense of the unskilled seasonal workers and their families. Today, many seasonal workers who do not qualify for an annual permit keep their families in secret, which is particularly damaging for school-age children.

Swiss nationals and those with unlimited residence permits have priority within the labour market. Behind them come the annual residents and, even further back, the seasonal workers. But worst off of all are the asylum-seekers, from countries like Turkey, Sri Lanka, Lebanon, Yugoslavia (Kosovo), Iran, Iraq, Angola and Zaire. They have to accept the jobs, of the most temporary nature, no one else wants. And they are the butt of racism. For, with the growth in Third World refugees in the 1980s has come an increase in those seeking asylum in Switzerland and, correspondingly, a growth in Swiss racism. Groups have sprung up like the commando-style Patriotic Front, or the apparently more respectable right-wing Action for Independent and Neutral Switzerland, under Christoph Blocher of the Swiss People's Party. These groups demand emergency legislation to stem all migration of refugees. In September 1990, six alleged members of the Patriotic Front were sentenced to prison for attacks in 1987 and 1989 on reception centres for asylum-seekers.

As pressure has increased from those seeking asylum, so Swiss policy on the issue has become increasingly restrictive. Before 1980, about 1,000 asylum-seekers came in a year, of whom about 80 per cent were recognised as refugees. Since that date, the numbers of those seeking asylum have steadily increased, yet the percentage of those given recognised status has steadily gone down. There are in Switzerland today over 40,000 asylum-seekers with applications pending and just over 29,000 officially recognised refugees. In 1989, only 197 were granted asylum and 12,708 asylum applications were refused; just over 700 would-be refugees were allowed residence permits out of overall quotas; 1,950 were allowed to stay for humanitarian reasons; 277 obtained a temporary stay order, and 347, mostly Tamils, were granted a temporary reprieve on their deportation. Such temporary acceptance of asylum-seekers and withholding of immediate deportation have been granted where people may be exposed to extreme violence and danger in their countries of origin. A number of residential permits, out of the regular quotas, and also those issued for 'humanitarian reasons' have been granted to help clear the backlog of asylum applications made years before. To deport these applicants after they have lived in the country this long would, in any case, smack of inordinate harshness and injustice. Conversely, the more the processing of asylum applications is streamlined and speeded up, the sooner could the number of applicants actually accepted as residents be further diminished.

As a consequence of the increase in the number of asylum-seekers, the originally liberal statutes governing asylum have been largely destroyed through various revisions of the law. In October 1988, a specially accelerated procedure for dealing with asylum-seekers was set in motion. It was extended in November 1989 to cover all asylum-seekers who had entered illegally from Yugoslavia, Pakistan, Turkey, Angola, Bangladesh, Ghana, Poland and Zaire – in other words, about 60 per cent of the total. Under this procedure, asylum applications are supposed to be dealt with and legally decided in a period of either three or five months. If asylum is refused, the applicant has five days before deportation (it was formerly six weeks). Some asylum-seekers are kept in special camps from their arrival right up to their deportation. Thus, they remain isolated both from the local population and from possible sources of help. It is a procedure which shows striking similarities with those of other western European countries (and some German Länder) which are designed to facilitate rapid deportation from major catchment centres.

In June 1990, asylum law was tightened further so as to impose the accelerated process on all refugees. A ban on employment was introduced for the first three months of asylum procedure. And asylum-seekers coming from countries where, in the opinion of the federal authorities, persecution does not exist will not be admitted. There will be no right of appeal and no access to any advisory body in such cases.

The Swiss asylum movement has long campaigned against the tightening of laws, demanding legal guarantees and safeguards to prevent anyone being forcibly returned to a country of arbitrary arrest, torture, assassination, etc. Furthermore, it demands that the concept of the refugee be widened to include all persons whose existence in their former country might be threatened, regardless of the nature of such a threat, whether from vendetta, death squads, civil wars and unrest, economic and social misery and pauperisation.

Of cardinal importance to the asylum movement is the demand for an economic policy, not only in Switzerland, but also in all industrialised countries, that would end the systematic exploitation of the Third World and thus obviate the real reasons for emigration and flight. It is clear that the growth in the number of refugees since 1980 has its roots in the growing indebtedness of the Third World, in the draconian economic measures forced on indebted nations, and in the growth of repression directed against their citizens.

Basle   JÜRG MEYER

Swedish racism: the democratic way

Traditionally, Sweden has never been much of a market for the lunatic fringe of the far Right. This is due not only to the fact that most Swedes – if we believe the opinion polls – take a rather dim view of extremist policies, but also because Sweden has enjoyed a comparatively stable growth of the economy for the past half century.

Not that Sweden has been without racists and fascists. There was a strong nazi undercurrent in the 'Golden Age of Fascism' in the 1930s, which had a distinct potential for expansion following the ascendancy of Hitler in 1933. However, the political interest of Sweden's working and middle class in those tumultuous years was turning to the labour movement and the Social Democratic Labour Party (SAP), whose policy formula of mixing trade unionism with a moderately progressive programme seemed like a far better deal. Hence, the fascist movement failed to build mass parties on the scale of its European counterparts.

After the Second World War, the bulk of the nazi Right melted away, leaving only a core of diehards. During the 1950s and 1960s, the picture remained unchanged: a handful of Old Guard veterans kept the boots polished, occasionally managing to attract the odd young recruit. The rest of the country paid little attention.

The fall and rise of racism
By the end of the 1960s, the Social Democrats, who had ruled Sweden for most of the previous sixty years, were at their peak. The growth of the economy had been staggering and the dream of the democratic 'welfare society' seemed to be within reach. The SAP leadership was gearing up to make Sweden internationally known as a model society: international solidarity and support for suffering Third World nations were election-winning political catchwords. Racism, most Swedes would seem to argue, was a thing of the ignorant past and fascism something that only happened elsewhere.

Immigration prior to 1970 was a minor issue, usually limited to other Europeans. Foreign workers, mostly Finns, Greeks and Yugoslavs, were encouraged to come to Sweden to fill the empty slots at

Volvo car factories and other large industries. Such immigrants generally had few problems in getting integrated and accepted in society at large – though they tended to stay at the bottom of the social ladder. There was only a small black population and little active racism – certainly, almost no organised violent racism.

Two decades later, much of this picture has changed. From the late 1960s onwards, Sweden began to attract a new form of immigrant. In 1967, the fascist coup in Greece caused the first exodus of political refugees to Sweden. Six years later, the Chilean coup marked the beginning of Latin American immigration, soon followed by Middle East and African refugees. During the 1980s, the country has seen an 'influx' of around 10,000 refugees per year.

By 1980, it was obvious that the traditional nazi movement – the left-overs from the 1940s – was politically obsolete. Three decades of ardent propaganda had left it with little success. Unable to win electoral support, even locally, the movement had regressed to a few isolated sects. To the young far-right activists this was a source of frustration, particularly so since the economic crisis and the increase of non-European immigrants seemed to open up new possibilities. The early 1980s saw a dramatic, if uncoordinated, increase in racist activities; but how to exploit the situation?

With a few notable exceptions – such as Per Engdahl, war-time führer and founder of the 1951 Malmö Brown International – Sweden's fascists have never acquired much prestige among fellow-travellers abroad. Partly as a result of this, there have been few serious political links to the international fascist movement. And yet, it was the developments abroad that gave a fillip to Sweden's racist Right. The 1970s had seen the growth of a strong nazi Right in Britain, a continued development of the militant movement in Italy and the early signs of the coming electoral success of the Front National in France. Terrorist outfits such as the Wehrsportsgruppe Hoffman in West Germany, Ordine Nuovo and, later, NAR in Italy, and FANE in France, had all made headlines in the Swedish media. To young activists inside as well as outside the traditional fascist groups, the rest of the continent became a source of inspiration.

The launching of the racist organisation Bevara Sverige Svenskt (BSS) (Keep Sweden Swedish) in 1980 was a decisive move: an attempt both to break away from the isolation of the traditional parties, and to rejuvenate the tarnished image of the extreme Right.*

* While only few details are known about the actual founding of the BSS, sources agree it was very much the brain-child of Leif Zeilon. Anti-fascists claimed he was a former activist of the Nordic Reich Party, a small but vocal gathering of diehard Hitlerites, but Zeilon, who recently changed his name to the more Swedish-sounding Ericsson, forcefully denies ever having been connected with the NRP.

The BSS was closely modelled on a British National Front blue-print. By keeping clear of traditional nazi symbols (swastikas, uni-forms, etc.), the BSS attempted to establish itself behind a clean and respectable façade. The official line promoted it as a democratic all-round political organisation for 'people concerned with Sweden's future', regardless of their party-political affiliations. While early members were recruited predominantly from traditional nazi outfits, the main effort was to attract followers from the less conspicuous mainstream of far-right activists. The BSS soon claimed supporters among all the regular parliamentary parties, including the Social Democrats and the Communists. The aim of this strategy, of course, was to attract ordinary conservative youths that the traditional lunatic fringe could not possibly hope to recruit. This master-plan partly fell through as the BSS soon began to issue membership cards to skinhead riff-raff and street thugs.

The fundamentals of the political message were also similar to those of the National Front: isolationism disguised as 'patriotism' or 'nationalism'; calls for law and order (the 'disorder' apparently being caused by immigrants); 'anti-communism'; a concern for environ-mental issues and, above all, an obsession with protecting Sweden's cultural heritage in the face of 'mass immigration'. Beyond the sometimes clever rhetoric, it was little more than the usual racist garbage.

Compared with earlier attempts to launch a broader fascist organis-ation, the BSS formula proved successful. By 1986, the BSS had a smooth political machinery, a regular paper and, most importantly, a seasoned activist cadre which already surpassed the traditional outfits. The exact membership figure is unknown, but including outside supporters it is estimated at a rough 500.* Then, in 1986, the BSS announced its sudden merger with another far-right organisation, Framstegspartiet (The Progress Party). At first, they looked like a pair of unlikely bedfellows.

Although ultra-rightist, the Progress Party was never seen as an outright fascist party, but rather as a nutty left-over from the fashionable populist movement that plagued the late 1960s. Formed originally in 1968, the Progress Party set out to build a Swedish version of the successful Danish party of the same name, run by Mogens Glistrup. Although initially it had attracted a handful of prominent mainstream conservatives, and built a respectable electoral following, its failure to win any seats in parliament in the 1970 election led to its stagnation. For almost fifteen years the party remained dormant, and, while participating in subsequent elections, never got even close to its

---

* As Sweden has only eight million citizens, this would translate to approximately 3,500 if compared with UK population figures.

initial success. To the public at large, it was a completely uninteresting far-right gathering until its merger with the BSS.

While surprising, there was no real reason why the Progress Party should not join forces with an openly racist group. Although the BSS was immensely more vocal and attracted much more media attention, both groups agreed on the basic question of immigration. And both groups had something to gain from the merger.

The Progress Party, on the one hand, had a much more developed and experienced organisation – a party structure – which was able to formulate a broader political programme. It knew how to participate in elections, run campaigns and even attract the floating voter. But it lacked a dedicated activist cadre to bring out its message. In the eyes of the Progress Party, the BSS possessed precisely those cadres of tough seasoned activists which could bring the party on to the streets.

To the BSS, on the other hand, the Progress Party offered a unique opportunity:
– First, the BSS gained access to a ready-made political party with experience from several election campaigns.
– Second, since the Progress Party was not immediately identified with uniformed loonies, the BSS would be able to draw even further away from the nazi Right, thus reinforcing its 'democratic' image.
– Finally, the BSS would not only triple its number of paying members, but also get access to the list of the Progress Party's fellow-travellers over the years – possibly as many as 10,000-15,000 – who might have an inclination for racist ideas.

As such, the merger was a very clever piece of political engineering by the BSS leadership which, in effect, simply hi-jacked the party it had merged with. The BSS did not mind that the chair of the Progress Party, Stefan Herrmann, became the first chair of the new party. He was a useful figurehead and the BSS, having made sure it held a majority vote in the party executive (five out of nine), was in a position to pull the strings. The new party became known as the Sverigepartiet (SP) (Sweden Party).

From street racism . . .
Shortly after the merger, SP activists and skinhead minders began making their presence felt in the streets. Party paper selling, leafleting and public meetings in key areas in downtown Stockholm became a common sight. Closet racists, who normally would not dare show up at a public meeting, suddenly found themselves cheering the SP along. By April 1987, the situation had deteriorated to the extent that the party had established what it considered 'its turf': left-wing paper sellers were eased out of their traditional spots and many immigrants were becoming increasingly uneasy about going past certain streets.

This was a display of force and a level of far-right activism unheard of since the war. More so; the SP was qualitatively different from any other recent fascist group. It had a young, determined cadre and a smooth and disciplined political machinery with a real potential for becoming a serious nuisance. Something clearly had to be done about them.

In April 1987, the national association Stop Racism agreed on a plan to counter the growth of the SP. To do so in a convincing manner, it argued, anti-fascists had to take on the SP on its own turf; to move the battle into the streets and reclaim lost areas. In short, it had to run the SP out of town. The strategy was simple: to ensure that the SP would be unable to hold one single public meeting undisturbed or unchallenged anywhere in Stockholm.

On 25 April, Stop Racism carried out its first counter-demonstration. The area selected was a tunnel walkway linking Stockholm railway station to the city underground – a narrow corridor strip where thousands of commuters pass daily and where SP activists and their skinhead minders had begun to appear regularly on Saturdays to sell their papers and harass passersby. At 10am on this Saturday morning, more than eighty anti-racists made their way into the passage, simply crowding the racists out. SP activists, outnumbered ten to one and unprepared for the sudden show of resistance, folded their business within minutes. This was the beginning of an anti-racist campaign which would run for seven months and end on the evening of 30 November.

The following Saturday, the SP marched into the tunnel with roughly 100 supporters, including a heavy guard of skinheads, only to find Stop Racism waiting for them with twice that number. This time the SP tried to hold its ground, but was again kicked out of the tunnel.

Within two weeks, the battle had moved from the crowded underground to the main streets of central Stockholm, with riot police trying to keep the two forces apart. As the scene was repeated every Saturday, support for the anti-racist campaign grew by the week. It soon included trade unions, immigrant organisations, churches and the general public. The first part of the campaign culminated on 6 June, Sweden's National Day, when more than 2,000 anti-racists took to the streets to dispose of SP activists at the main square in central Stockholm.

By this time panic was mounting within the ranks of the SP. In spite of heavy internal mobilisation, fewer and fewer racists felt inclined to take a whipping every Saturday. The spirit of the party had been broken.

During the summer holidays, outside support for the campaign cooled off, but activists of Stop Racism kept up the protests.

Sometimes only a mere dozen activists turned out, but numbers no longer counted. The idea was to keep up pressure on the SP and force it into a state of constant mobilisation.

By October, tension began increasing again. For years, it has been the habit of veteran fascists to commemorate the death of Sweden's eighteenth-century warrior King Karl XII on 30 November. This used to be a small and insignificant occasion, but with the arrival of the BSS, it had become the single most important far-right rally of the year, often involving several hundred fascist marchers in Stockholm and the southern town of Lund.

For the SP, this was to be the day when it would get its revenge for the humiliating defeat of the summer. It obtained the necessary police permits and mobilised its activists. And, on the day, it was allowed to gather unchallenged at its point of assembly: a large square in a fashionable part of the city which, however, can only be entered by way of a few narrow streets. But the square was also a trap. At the moment the march was about to begin, hundreds of anti-fascists sealed the square by blocking the narrow streets. The police, suddenly realising they had a 'situation' at hand, hastily erected riot fences around the square.

It became an extremely humiliating evening for the Master Race. After three hours – at -15° C with a north wind blowing – it became obvious that the anti-fascists would not allow the march to take place, so the chief constable revoked the permit and told the SP activists to go home.

. . . to respectable racism

The November fiasco spelled disaster for the extravagant plans of the SP: the dream of launching a Republikaner type of party which could bring together the racist Right in the forthcoming general elections. It believed the time was right for a new political force, nourished by a common discontent with the politics of the established parties. The strategists of the SP were careful to reject officially racism and nazi associations. However, victims of skinhead attacks or parents of adopted children – who were told that all non-European immigrants who had arrived later than 1965 would be repatriated – had few doubts about the real character of the party.

For a brief time the SP seemed to have a real opportunity to establish itself as a small but serious factor in the far right field. By December 1987, that moment had already passed and that failure was to a large part due to the campaign of Stop Racism. From April to November, while the meetings of the SP were continuously disrupted, it was impossible to undertake any serious public activity. Shortly after this debacle, the SP split under its own inherent contradictions. The former BSS faction, regrouped as the Sweden Democrats and, launched in Spring 1988, are now the most effective of Sweden's far-right sects. By the end of 1989, the number of recruits had tripled and from figures obtained in mid-1990, its membership is now estimated to be 4,000. During the same time, the Sweden Democrats have established local party branches in around thirty cities – an unparalleled expansion in far-right terms.

While the party is much less visible in terms of street activity than was the SP, it has found other outlets for its propaganda. It has weekly broadcasts on the Stockholm Community Network (local radio open to any political group or religious congregation) and issues a monthly journal, the Sweden Courier. It apparently has wide-ranging links to some fascist groups in Europe, such as the National Front and the British National Party in the UK, Front National in France, the *Republikaner* in Germany, as well as the up-market far-right journal the *Scorpion* published in Germany by former NF member Michael Walker, though these connections are rarely visible in its official propaganda.

The Sweden Democrats' new line calls for grassroot party building at local level. Today, skinheads are out of fashion, unless they conform to the new suit and tie image of up-to-date racists. The core of the party executive, however, remains essentially the same, with at least three of its nine members being former leaders of the BSS. It plans to participate in the 1991 general elections in Sweden, and stands a serious chance of actually winning one or two seats in local assemblies. It should be noted that although the party did not participate formally in the 1988 election – due to the SP debacle – nevertheless, it won about 1,100 stray votes – the largest post-war vote for a far-right party in Sweden.

Racism by referendum
But it is not only through the activities of far-right groups like the Sweden Democrats that race has come onto the political agenda, though their grassroots local work has undoubtedly heightened the issue. It has also emerged in mainstream politics, most dramatically during the 1988 elections when Sven-Olle Olsson, a local chairman of the mainstream Centre Party in the small southern parish of Sjöbo, rebelled against the party line and called for a local referendum to refuse shelter to political refugees in the parish. The Sjöbo referendum made headlines and put the small town, with a population of only a few thousand, in the international limelight.

Sjöbo became important because, for the first time, a respected mainstream politician was exploiting anti-immigration sentiments with the arguments of the racist Right. (In fact, a leading member of the New Swedish Movement was invited to write a pamphlet on the issue for the Sjöbo Centre Party.) The ensuing debate became an embarrassment for the Centre Party, one of Sweden's largest parties, which had led the government between 1976 and 1982.

The party leaders attempted, unsuccessfully, to cancel the referendum. In the process, Olsson, who was swiftly expelled from the party, became a sympathetic and popular figure. The Sjöbo referendum was won by a landslide and Swedish politics changed fundamentally, almost overnight.

Of course, racist and neo-fascist groups, such as the Sweden Democrats and the Nordic Reich Party, cheered the outcome of the Sjöbo referendum. At last, they argued, the voice of the ordinary Swedish citizen was heard, and that voice called for an end of the swamping of Sweden by foreign elements.

The racist Right, particularly the Sweden Democrats, have been able to exploit the Sjöbo referendum to the hilt, calling for a similar referendum at the national level. The current strategy is to phrase the demand, not in terms of racism or immigration, but as a question of 'local democracy', where 'ordinary people' can have a say in an increasingly controversial issue.

Already the racist Right has carried out successful campaigns in various areas where political refugee centres are being planned. This is the case in Kimstad, a small town with a population of a thousand, where the Sweden Democrats have been very active since it was announced that an abandoned building would be rebuilt to shelter 175 political refugees. As in Sjöbo, the campaign won the support of two mainstream politicians, this time from Moderaterna, Sweden's conservative party. For a while it seemed as if Kimstad would be transformed into a new Sjöbo; however, once the political refugees actually arrived, tensions in fact diminished.

Following the Sjöbo referendum, there has been a visible increase in racial violence, particularly attacks all over Sweden against refugee centres. In 1989, more than a dozen serious attacks, including the use of petrol bombs and arson, were carried out. The attacks continued in 1990, culminating in a week-long blitz against refugee centres at the end of May. Eleven people were injured and property valued close to £1m was destroyed in the attacks, which included the use of bombs, arson and poison gas.

– The Kungälv refugee centre was wrecked by heavy dynamite blast; miraculously its 130 guests escaped unharmed.

– Two buildings in the Kimstad refugee centre were gutted by fire only one week before the arrival of 175 refugees.

– The newly built refugee centre in Mariestad was torched only 24 hours before the first refugees were to arrive.

– The remote Bocksjön refugee centre was the scene of an attack where two men hurled a military smoke grenade into the main building, poisoning eleven people who needed medical treatment for

respiratory problems.
– In Laholm, fifteen fully-equipped cabins, which had been offered by their owner to be used as refugee centres, were torched. Racist slogans such as 'No Niggers in Laholm' had been daubed nearby.
– In Västerås, three petrol bombs were set off at a refugee centre where fifty were staying. Nobody was injured.

In all, about twenty violent attacks were carried out during 1990. Though no fascist group claimed responsibility, Swedish anti-racists have pointed out that the Sweden Democrats have carried out overt propaganda campaigns in most of these areas. Few arrests have been made, but in two cases arrests have linked members of the Hitlerite Nordic Reich Party to attacks, and in one case a supporter of the Sweden Democrats.

The Sjöbo referendum, as well as the wave of attacks on political refugees, are both signs of increased racism among sections of the Swedish population and a hardening of attitude towards immigrants. Already the government is showing signs of backing down from its traditional liberal attitude towards refugees.

Sweden's quota of refugees stands at 20,000 a year, but, according to government figures, the number arriving during the autumn of 1989 was twice as high. As a result, it decided late in 1989 to introduce new and far stricter immigration rules.

Under the new regulations, political asylum will be granted only to individuals who fit the exact letter of the United Nations Refugee Charter, instead of, as previously, according to its spirit. If these changes had been in operation in 1988, only about 25 per cent of those who applied for refugee status would have qualified. Ms Maj-Lis Lööw, who is the Social Democrat minister of immigration, justified the change in policy by claiming that the Swedish Immigration Board could no longer handle the 'flood of refugees' and that there was no room left in the country's refugee centres.

That decision, made without reference to either the Swedish parliament or to the Social Democrat party grassroots, led to a public outcry. Experts on the refugee situation as well as church authorities protested loudly at the measures.

The controversy became increasingly sharp during Christmas 1989, when the government announced that 5,000 Bulgarian Turks were among those who would not be considered political refugees. The deportation of twenty of them sparked immediate protests. At one refugee camp, 500 awaiting a decision from the immigration authorities, barricaded themselves in. At the same time, the Greens, the Left Party and the Liberals jointly established a committee against the legislation, which was soon supported by an impressive number of bodies, including the Lutheran Church of Sweden, the Roman Catholic Church, Amnesty International and the Refugee Council.

By New Year's Eve, dozens of Swedish churches were occupied by refugees and protesting Swedes. The occupations were carried out with the full support of the local priests, including Swedish Archbishop Bertil Werkström. Nonetheless, the minister of immigration stated that the new rules would not be re-negotiated. The occupations of churches went on well into March 1990, when they finally came to an end in the face of the government's stubborn refusal to negotiate. As I write, the new regulations are still in operation, although the issue is by no means settled.

Stockholm   STIEG LARSSON

Norway's national racism

The presence of black people in the Scandinavian countries is quite recent; the injustice and discriminatory mechanisms they are subject to has, however, a long history behind it. Norway has never had colonies – although it has benefited (indirectly) from the colonial system, and imbibed racist theories from colonial Europe.

Until recently, Norway was a country of massive emigration. Between 1865 and 1915, for instance, three-quarters of a million people went to the United States.* For much of this period – up till 1905, in fact – the country was under Swedish and Danish domination. The struggle for building a nation state has, however, had its price, most of which was paid by the indigenous Lappish people in the north – or Samis, as they prefer to be called. Sami religion, language and right to land was ruthlessly suppressed. The 'Norwegianisation' of the Samis is still a recent memory. But also seen as a danger to the emerging Norwegian nation were Finnish migrants who had been travelling between Finland and Norway for centuries. The nation-building process exposed racist tendencies.

During the Second World War, Jews and gypsies were victimised. So hated was Norway's collaborationist government under Major Quisling that it gave a new word to the English language. It is interesting to note the similarities between statements made by officials on Third World immigrants today and by officials in the 1930s and 1940s against the Jews.

It was after the Second World War that the need to import labour power was first felt. For, however peripheral and poor Norway was until the end of the Second World War, it was, after all, still a part of

---

* The population of Norway today, approximately four million, is still less than the number of Norwegians living in the US.

Europe. So it benefited from the Marshall Plan, which put it on course for rapid development. The first workers to be brought in were Italians, most of whom left the country in the 1960s. (Though, even today, the echoes of shouts of 'dagoes' may still break the silence of snowfall at a train station.)

The second major factor in Norway's economic development was the discovery of oil in the North Sea. Workers were needed, yelled the daily ads in the Middle Eastern and other overseas newspapers. They were wanted not only in the off-shore oil industry, but also in timber and steel and, not least, to take on the unwanted jobs in the service industries. The first immigrants from the Third World started coming in the late 1960s, but more arrived in the 1970s. (Before then, there had been only a few dozen black people living in Norway.) Reasons were many, but restrictions in Germany and the 1970 ban on immigration in Denmark were the main factors in the move northwards. Seven Pakistani workers arrived one winter night at the border. The border guard was drunk, he undid his tie and threw it towards them: 'Those of you who can tie this tie can stay.' Three of them came across the border. Once a person got work, to get a work permit was not difficult.

This laissez-faire period, however, was over by 1975, when the first immigration ban was introduced, not, ostensibly, to stop immigrants, but 'to make conditions better for those who had already arrived'. The conditions never got better, but the ban remained. Its true function was to maintain state control over the influx of labour; it was a mediating instrument for government between the trade unions and the employers and was racist in that it was aimed directly at people from the Third World.

By the end of 1975, when the ban was introduced, the total number of people originating from the Third World (including children born in Norway to 'immigrant' parents) was 37,500 – less than the number of residents from North America and other European countries. Despite this, however, the government still expressed fear (as in the green paper of 1980) that Norway would continue to attract large scale migration from countries in the Third World and Turkey. The paper introduced a discriminatory policy of control over people from the Third World. A new law – introduced in 1983, but not put into practice until 1989 – legitimised the discriminatory practices and mechanisms of the immigration ban. The effects of this policy were obvious – it is not just a coincidence that, until April 1984, two different employment offices existed in Oslo, only one of which was open to immigrants. The message of the 1975 ban was clear: immigration was a problem.

The extreme Right was quick to make the connection between immigration as a problem and immigrants as a threat. The history of the Nazi-oriented Right in Norway goes back to the 1930s. The Nazi occupation of Norway left traumatic memories, yet the ideology underlying this experience has hardly ever been challenged – seeing the war veterans from the resistance movement now active in anti-immigrant organisations is enough to illustrate this. It also sheds light on another tragic fact – that most of the resistance in Europe against the German occupation was nationalist rather than anti-fascist.

'Nasjonal Ungdomsfylking', from the late 1960s, and 'Moderat Ungdom', from the early 1970s, are both youth organisations which gave birth to the NF, the Norwegian Front, with its clear Nazi orientation. The NF came to an end, however, when some of its active members were prosecuted after a bomb was thrown into a workers' demonstration on 1 May 1979. The NF leader, Eric Blucher, moved to Brighton in Sussex, from where, in 1980, he helped start a new organisation active in Norway, the largely clandestine National People's Party. In 1983, the NPP shocked the country with its threats of violence if black children joined the annual children's parade on the national day. In 1986, however, five active members were jailed after being found guilty of a bomb explosion in a mosque in Oslo in June 1985.

1983 was also an important year, not only because 'immigrants' got voting rights in the municipal elections, but also because the first anti-racist group in Scandinavia, started in 1978, managed to establish the Antirasistisk-Senter. This resource centre today runs a magazine, *Samora*, and puts out local radio transmissions in seven languages. It has a library, archives on the extreme Right, develops multimedia resources for youth clubs, schools and trade unions, and also has an emergency counselling group. The centre has initiated the youth movement, SOS Racism, which operates today not only independently of the centre but, more importantly, independently of SOS Racism in France. SOS Racism's seventy local branches all over the country have offered a challenge to growing racist organisations.

Since 1987, racism has escalated in Norway for mainly two reasons. Until 1987, there was a certain consensus among the parliamentary parties on immigration policies. In the general elections of 1987, that consensus was broken by the Progress Party, a populist party which wanted to make 'too many immigrants in the country' a national issue. The lack of debate on such issues in national forums, where people could take part, had left the field clear for the racist organisations to work at manipulating local communities. The Progress Party managed to cash in on the prejudice that had been built up. It increased its presence in the parliament to 12 per cent, giving new life to extreme Right groups and legitimising attacks on black people on the streets and at work. The ground work for this development had been done, however, by the state agencies in their policies on immigration and refugees.

The policy of the Norwegian state towards refugees is a textbook example of shame and scandal. Its major contribution has been to turn refugees and asylum-seekers into social welfare clients, a burden on any local community into which they have been randomly thrown. And the extreme Right has played up this situation to its own benefit. Racist activities, once limited to clandestine groups, have become the fashion for many today. Popular racist organisations, such as the People's Movement Against Immigration and Stop Immigration, with its former war veterans as members, recruit both from left and right political parties. What was once a criminal act, for racist groups to appear in public, is now legitimate and to hinder it is called 'limiting the freedom of speech'.

The struggle against racism has been gathering strength through immigrants' national organisations, youth organisations, the Antirasistisk Senter, SOS Racism's local branches and spontaneous activities to support the victims of racism as well as to challenge the racists. Regular rallies and mobilisations are common in many cities in Norway. The movement, however, has to ask of itself: how to convey to Norwegian society at large the reality of racism as corrosive of the nation, and the fight against racism as its proper zeitgeist.

Antirasistisk-Senter, Oslo   KHALID SALIMI

Denmark: no racism by definition

To judge by the courts' rulings on racial incitement and racial slurs, one would think that there was no such thing as racism in Denmark. For, although there is one small proviso in the statute books (s266b of the penal code) which makes racial slurs punishable in law, the courts have generally held that the term racism could only be used to mean the belief that one's own race is superior to all others – the so-called 'scientific' definition. Thus, although the courts were prepared to invoke s266b in the case of two TV journalists who televised the racist slurs made by young racist thugs (the Green Jackets), no action was taken, for example, against a member of the Danish Society who sent a letter to all members of Copenhagen city council, calling for a 'public bloodbath' to stave off the 'Mohammedan invasion'. The police, in fact, refused to prosecute.

Indeed, the courts have gone so far as to declare it a criminal libel to call Danish society racist.

But Denmark, like most European countries, spans the whole

spectrum of racism, ranging from the usual stereotyping of non-white immigrants as hordes of foreigners overrunning a virgin land, through the stigmatising of their cultures (especially Islam) as alien and threatening, to, finally, the institutionalised racism of the police, the immigration authorities, the municipal councils, etc.

The newspapers are full of such stereotyping – in their articles, in their editorials, on their letters pages. Reading them, one would soon conclude that Denmark was overrun with foreigners who are all to blame for Denmark's real economic problems. Studies have shown that more than 70 per cent of all newspaper coverage on foreigners in Denmark is concerned either with crime or with social problems. Frequently, such coverage is not only exaggerated and distorted, but contains out-and-out lies. Nor is this true only of the letters pages, which are often full of material from the far Right. One of the worst examples was a series of twenty-three articles in one newspaper, *BT*, under the title 'Them and us'. A critical publication, *Press*, revealed that out of the twenty-three articles, more than twenty contained misleading information and direct falsehoods.

And, of course, throughout such coverage it is, as often as not, not just the individual foreigner who stands accused but the whole race, religion, culture which is condemned. Less than 3 per cent of Denmark's population are foreign nationals, and, of these, over half are from other European countries, Canada, Australia or the US. But it is the 'Muslim invasion' that is spoken of, the 'cultural threat from the Third World'.

It is quite clear that Muslims, who have been called 'the arsenic in pure Danish water' (Glistrup, founder of the Progress Party), are the main target of this smear campaign. And the generalisations do not stop at making all Muslims accomplices in that which an individual Muslim commits. Islam, in its own right, is attacked in racial slurs reminiscent of anti-Semitism in the 1930s. The proposed erection of a mosque would be 'a monument to male chauvinism', according to one woman member of the Danish Society. Or, again, Islam is 'a religion out of the middle ages', in the words of one local mayor, who also stated that 'Musselmen keep their women prisoner'.

Institutionalised racism
Possibly even more serious than such blatant stereotyping, however, is the institutionalisation of racism in Denmark. There is no space for a systematic survey, but the following are examples drawn from several different areas. Take, for example, the police, whose racism is frequently backed up by the courts. One policeman, who shot and killed an unarmed Palestinian refugee, got off scot free by pleading self-defence – on the grounds that he thought the Palestinian was preparing to take up a karate position. But an Iranian refugee who

stabbed and killed an off-duty policeman, who had chased him for several blocks for no apparent reason, was given life imprisonment.

Or, recently, a Tanzanian man was sent 'home' to Kenya(!) because of a police blunder: they thought he was seeking asylum, when in fact he only wanted to visit his fiancée. The man's papers were in order and he had a legal right to visit Denmark as a tourist. Apparently, it never occurred to them to get hold of an interpreter. A similar incident happened to a man from Gambia. He had his hand broken by the police, who arrested him for trying to enter the country. His papers, too, were in order. And, once again, the police failed to call in an interpreter.

More generally, blacks are subject to arbitrary police behaviour. In Copenhagen, for example, they are often frisked, harassed, arrested and told to stay away from public places. Reason? The suspicion that some Gambians are involved in dope smuggling.

Racism reaches throughout the prison system too. A pair of male nurses who had said that the majority of prison guards in a Danish prison had racist tendencies, were initially charged with libel, but were acquitted. For the judge found their case proven, their statement correct.

But institutionalised racism also takes place on a much higher level. Officials in the justice department purposely delayed some Tamils' applications to get close relatives out of Sri Lanka and into Denmark. The Danish Immigration Act states quite clearly that foreigners who have residence permits have an unconditional right to bring their spouses and children under 18 years of age into the country. But the authorities withheld approval without just cause and delayed the cases as long as possible. At least one of the dependants was killed before the approval came through.

And in two counties, Ishoej and Randers, the communal authorities have – with no legal justification – refused to let flats to foreigners. The reason given was that one foreign family already lived in the building in question and that the county wanted to avoid ghettoes!

The rise of the far Right
Not surprisingly, the general climate of racism has given a boost to the far-right movement, which in turn has exploited and exacerbated popular racism and stereotyping – and, in the process, shifted mainstream politics to the right.

One of the most active and significant of such groups is the Danish Society, whose aim is to kick all foreigners out of Denmark (with the exception of executives of multinational companies). The Danish Society has specialised in hate campaigns against immigrants and refugees; most of all, it despises Muslims. It is led by professional academics and two priests, but most of its members are pensioners, shopkeepers, artisans and disgruntled workers. What is particularly significant about the Danish Society is the privileged status it enjoys in a large section of the Danish press. Not only does it publish its own monthly magazine *Danskeren* (*The Dane*) (which recently contained passages of barely concealed incitements to violence), but it gets a wide airing for such views throughout the rest of the media. It has developed an organised campaign to swamp newspapers with letters to the editor urging 'a stop to this criminal invasion of our land'. Of late, this campaign has become more aggressive, urging Danes to undertake 'active opposition' to the 'invasion'.

Continual propaganda from groups such as the Danish Society has had a significant effect in influencing several newspapers to take a fiercely anti-immigrant stand. A vicious spiral is established. An anti-immigration lobby creates a demand which is supplied by the newspapers, who then can sell more newspapers by creating a demand which is supplied by the rabid anti-immigration lobby.

The Danish Society, though, does not stand alone. Smaller groupings are:

– *DNSB* (the Nazis). Its number of members is not known and – nominally – it is without political influence. But DNSB has widespread contacts on the international level with other extreme rightwing groups.

– *The National Party*. This is a neo-fascist party, which was even in the ballot in two or three communities in the local elections two years ago. The Nationalists have made public threats against some prominent immigrants. It has been questioned whether they were connected with or responsible for an attack against an immigrant politician from the Socialist Peoples Party and a member of the Copenhagen City Council.

– *The Ku Klux Klan (Danish chapter)* hardly needs further introduction. It is a marginal group, but last summer the police uncovered a vast arsenal in a house belonging to one of its leading members.

Of much greater significance, however, is the fact that a number of political parties have made racism an integral part of their platform. Racism has, in effect, been forced into the mainstream of Danish political life. The least successful of these in electoral terms is the Citizens List: Stop Immigration. It consists of ex-local leaders of the Danish Society, the Progress Party and the Nazis. It had candidates in four major cities in the 1989 local elections, but obtained no more than 5,868 votes. Nonetheless, its vociferous leaders are active in the media, denouncing immigrants and refugees, deriding their culture and screaming for the establishment of apartheid in Denmark.

Far more important is the Progress Party. Originally a populist, anti-tax protest party, it has slowly evolved into an arch right-wing movement. Capital punishment, economic Darwinism, more power

to and less control over the police, and cutting of social benefit are all
part of its programme. It also calls for 'a Denmark with no Musselmen'. Various spokesmen for the party have also called Muslims 'mad
dogs' and have said that 'immigrants' proliferate 'like rats'. Its leader
and founder, Mogens Glistrup, has said that he would vote against
granting Danish citizenship to Muslims.

The Progress Party has at the moment sixteen seats (out of 189) in
parliament. But, according to the polls, it could get as many as twenty
five in the next election. This has forced Denmark's Liberal Party to
try to beat the Progress Party at its own game. The Liberals, who have
twenty-two seats at the present, and are in the coalition government,
are trying to be even more anti-tax and almost as anti-immigrant as the
Progress Party. And, with this stance, it, too, is expecting huge gains in
the next election.

There have, however, been some setbacks to the far-right racist
lobby. In March 1990, an attempt was made to unify all the anti-
immigrant groups. The attempt failed because the city council in
Fredericka, where the meeting was to be held, refused permission for
it and the hotel-owners cancelled the booking when they found out the
nature of the meeting. This effort at unification was the culmination of
the past ten years growing anti-immigrant, anti-refugee and anti-
Muslim propaganda. Nor will it be the last.

But, far from meeting this right-wing challenge head on, most
politicians have either ignored it or, as in the case of the Liberals, have
even tried to capitalise on the prejudices aroused. For, as one
politician who has the courage of her convictions put it: 'The problem
for professional politicians is, there are no votes to win, but an awful
lot of votes to lose' (Birthe Weiss, vice-forewoman in the Social
Democrats, Denmark's largest party).

Racial violence
So far, there have not been the widespread violent confrontations in
Denmark that have taken place elsewhere in Europe. But the
situation is getting tense, and many 'foreigners' live in constant fear.
Immigrant-owned shops are attacked. Their clubs and homes are
ransacked. Their children are harassed in schools. Some immigrants
have even been killed. And there have been sporadic incidents where
refugee camps have been attacked by angry mobs. The worst took
place about five years ago in the coastal city of Kalundborg.

A member of the Copenhagen city council was attacked in the
daytime outside her home and hospitalised. An organisation named
'The White Hand' was apparently responsible, but no arrests have
been made. Nor have there been any arrests over incidents where
several shots were fired into a barracks where refugees slept, or where
an incendiary bomb was thrown into a refugee centre, or where a

children's club was set on fire in the North Zeeland city of Frederiks-vaerk.

Unlike France, Great Britain and Germany, there is no real skinhead movement. There is, however, an organised group of youths who are often referred to as Green Jackets (because they wear ex-US pilot jackets). These youths have been involved in numerous attacks on immigrants and refugees, who are the Green Jackets' favourite, but by no means only, target. Ironically, these Green Jackets are – like their victims – only interesting when they commit crimes. They – again often like their victims – tend to be unemployed, unskilled, uns-chooled and without much real hope of improving upon their bleak future. The police do little and seem to care less about such incidents – including that in which the co-author of this article had a gun pointed at his head and was told to leave the country.

Fortunately, there is still a majority in the Danish parliament who take human rights and civil rights seriously. And they see it as their responsibility to ensure that the democratic system works. But the Liberal Party and the Progress Party are hungry for power. They are competing with one another to satisfy a growing populist and racist opinion. And, if they succeed in pulling the Conservative Party along with them, they will be able to muster a racist majority. Then the old Bob Dylan song 'I pity the poor immigrant' will take on a whole new meaning.

Copenhagen   BASHY QURAISHY and TIM O. CONNOR

Holland: the bare facts

Immigration
About 4 per cent of the population of 15 million in Holland are 'immigrants' or their children. Numbering 190,000, the Surinamese (from the former Dutch colony of Surinam in South America) form the largest 'immigrant' group in Holland. Next come the Turks, with 160,000, and the Moroccans, with 120,000. There are 50,000 Dutch Antilleans from the Caribbean. The Moluccans from the Indonesian island of Molucca number around 40,000, as do the gypsies. The other 'immigrant' groups, from Latin America, Africa, Asia, the Middle East and the Mediterranean, vary between a few thousand to 10,000. Immigrants from the rich EC countries (Germany, Belgium, France, UK, Italy, Ireland and Luxembourg) are normally not viewed as immigrants or included in the discussion on them, although, at 161,000, they are larger than the Turkish group.

Indo-Europeans

Immigration to Holland started after the Second World War. The first large group of immigrants were the Indo-Europeans who left Indonesia after decolonisation, considering themselves as more closely attached to the Netherlands than to Indonesia. Most of them appeared to be white rather than black and integration into Dutch society was straightforward. Nor were they considered a special target of state policy towards minorities, since they neither presented themselves nor were seen as different from the Dutch. This group is estimated at around 200,000.

Moluccans

The Moluccans were part of the colonial army fighting the Indonesians. When it became clear that Indonesians would be victorious in their fight for independence and to establish their own republic, the Dutch transferred the demobilised Moluccan soldiers to barracks in the Dutch countryside. The Moluccans were promised by the Dutch that an agreement would soon be reached with the Indonesians which would enable them to return to an independent republic of South Molucca. Until that time, they were to remain in camps in Holland, where a government-in-exile was formed. Year after year the Dutch reneged on their promise, and eventually – after serious confrontations in Holland with the Moluccan community (which included the hijacking of trains and violent demonstrations for an independent South Molucca) – an agreement was reached in the 1980s between the Dutch government and the Moluccan leaders. By this agreement, the Dutch were freed of their commitment to press for an independent republic of South Molucca in exchange for a programme enabling the Moluccans to leave the camps and integrate into the labour market. One of the requirements of this policy was an affirmative action programme to bring 1,000 Moluccans into government service. The programme did not fully materialise.

Guest workers

At the end of the 1950s and during the 1960s, the industrialisation of Holland expanded rapidly, and Dutch industry needed workers. Thousands of immigrants were recruited from the Mediterranean countries, especially Turkey and Morocco, for manual labour, but the economic crises of the 1970s brought this process to an end. The so-called guest workers lost their jobs and were pressured to leave. Some did go, but others staged a successful fight for the right to stay.

Surinamese

The Dutch colonies of Surinam and the Antilles in the Caribbean also provided Holland with workers in the 1950s and 1960s. Racial tensions and economic crises led to large emigration from Surinam in the 1970s.

Government policy
Initially, government policy towards immigrants was based on the assumption that they were here only temporarily. After earning enough money, the urge to leave for the homeland would ensure a return-migration. The organisation and encouragement of this cycle was the cornerstone of government policy. Thus, while welfare organisations were subsidised to assist immigrants in getting proper housing and a place in the labour market, they were also giving out information on how 'immigrants' could return to their country of birth on an assisted repatriation scheme.

By the end of the 1970s, it became clear that the 'immigrants' were here to stay. But the economic crisis of the 1970s had also started a process of restructuring in Dutch industry. Automation and computerisation had led to the discarding of unskilled labour from the economy and to a rise in the service sector. 'Immigrants' were becoming unemployed on a large scale.

Government policy now shifted from a policy of return-migration, which did not work, to that of integrating immigrants in Dutch society along the lines of 'integration with preservation of cultural identity'. The promotion of racial harmony, multicultural events and awareness training within white institutions were to follow.

Politics
The same period also saw fascist and racist political parties making gains. In 1982, a party which campaigned openly against immigrants was elected into parliament. In all large cities these parties have gained seats in local government.

In 1986, legal 'immigrants' were given the right to vote in local government elections, and some forty were elected in different cities. All major political parties (especially the Social Democrats and the Christian Democrats) have non-white candidates who campaign in their communities.

In the media, trade unions, educational institutions and other sectors of society, there is a slow growth of an 'immigrant' presence.

Labour market
Unemployment is the most serious problem for non-white communities. Whilst the unemployment rate amongst the Dutch is 13 per cent, for 'immigrants' the rate varies between 23 per cent (for the Antilleans) to 44 per cent (for Turks). The educational level of 'immigrants' is lower than that of Dutch workers, and even in unskilled work, doors

are often closed to non-whites. Those with educational qualifications comparable to whites find it harder to compete for skilled occupations.

Among young 'immigrants', there is a large group who feel they will never find a job on the regular labour market. Discussion on labour market policy concentrates on the extent to which unemployment should be attributed to poor education or to racism. If it should prove a matter of poor educational levels, labour market policy should concentrate on that; if racism, then labour market policy should examine how far programmes of affirmative action should be introduced (e.g., contract compliance, positive action). Initially, government policy was based on the first premise, but since it is clear that, despite a rise in the educational level, unemployment is still rampant, there is an attempt to introduce some kind of positive action programme. The scientific council for government policy, an official advisory board to the government, recently proposed the introduction of a law on equal treatment of 'immigrants', according to which major companies would have to publish a yearly report detailing what efforts were made to attract 'immigrant' workers. There is also pressure for stronger measures.

Housing
The concentration of non-whites in urban areas in the west of the country brings another dimension to the 'immigrant' question. About 50 per cent of the 'immigrants' live in the four largest cities (Amsterdam, The Hague, Rotterdam and Utrecht), where they constitute from 15-20 per cent of the total population.

They are concentrated in the old districts where social services are poor, and in some areas they form a majority of the population. One debate now going on is whether housing associations and the municipal authorities should provide a form of segregated housing, with special blocks for specific ethnic groups. A survey conducted by the Warray Research Institute among white and non-white residents of two districts in The Hague showed that a majority of people living in these districts did not favour the idea of segregated districts with small Chinatowns, Turkeytowns, etc.

Warray Research Institute, Hague   SANDEW HIRA

Addendum: racial incidents
According to the Anne Frank Foundation, Amsterdam, the following incidents took place in 1986:

2 February: Some 40 graves are destroyed in a Jewish cemetery in Amersfoort. The police do not think 'anti-Semitism' is the motive. (*Source:* Volkskrant)

19 February: A shopkeeper from Meppel, who was cooperating with other shopkeepers in order to cut down shoplifting, declared that 'in particular, foreigners without residence permits are potential thieves'. A complaint was filed against him by the Moroccan Association. (*Source:* Nieuwsblad voor het Noorden)

April: A 37-year-old Antillean was shot in his home by a policeman. The police had been warned that a fight was going on in the man's home. When they arrived, the fight was already over. The man refused to allow the police to enter his home. A fight broke out, a shot was fired, and the man was hit.(*Source:* Waarheid)

11 April: In the Hague, a 40-year-old man from Surinam was killed by a police bullet. According to the police, the man threatened a police officer with a kitchen knife. According to the family of the victim, the police fired without any obvious reason. The policeman was not prosecuted because, according to the Public Prosecutor, he acted in self-defence. (*Source:* Volkskrant)

13 May: In Hilversum, an 18-year-old youth was threatened with a gun because of the colour of his skin. The boy recognised his assailant from a police photograph. His assailant was subsequently arrested. (*Source:* Gooi en Eemlander)

20 May: Two men from the Hoekse Waard were arrested by the police because they had twice beaten up and tried to rob foreigners. They told the police that they went to Rotterdam especially to beat up foreigners. (*Source:* Trouw)

22 May: On a Sunday night in May, an 18-year-old girl was severely mistreated in Castricum by four boys. They carved SS and a swastika on to her skin. The four boys drove mopeds and pulled the girl off her bike. The signs were cut in so deep that they will remain scars. (*Source:* Volkskrant)

31 May: 'Get lost filthy Turk', a young man threatened a 13-year-old boy of Turkish origin who had been watching him clean the exhaust of his car for a little while. The boy reacted and the young man pushed a burning newspaper into his face and then ran off. The burns had to be treated in hospital. (*Source:* Utrechts Nieuwsblad)

May: A council member of Amsterdam, Mrs Tara Oedayaraj Singh Varma, was threatened several times over the phone. She was told 'filthy Jew, we'll gas you' and 'we don't want any foreigners in the council, we want you to resign'. She went into hiding for a time. (*Source:* Telegraaf)

14 July: In Amsterdam, an empty building which was to become the community centre of a Surinam Cultural Association was set on fire. Rumours had spread that drugs were being sold there. (*Source:* Parool)

11 August: A bomb exploded in a Turkish coffee house in Schiedam. Nobody was hurt, but the front of the building was destroyed. The Young Persons

Front of Schiedam claimed responsibility. The police arrested three young men. An 18-year-old youth was convicted and sentenced to one-and-a-half-year's imprisonment. The others were sentenced to twelve and five months, respectively. (*Source:*Volkskrant)

25 August: An attempt was made to set the mosque of Deventer on fire. Only the quick reaction of the fire brigade prevented extensive damage. At the same time, stones were thrown through the windows of Turkish shops. The stones were marked with swastikas. The offenders, two servicemen, were arrested in November. (*Source:* Trouw)

September: On 3 September, prior to the football match between Ajax Amsterdam and FC The Hague, several football supporters of FC The Hague were heard shouting anti-Semitic slogans. The police refused to act. On 14 September, a supporter of FC The Hague was arrested for giving the Hitler salute. (*Source:* Trouw)

29 September: A 27-year-old man from Hilversum killed a Moroccan. The killer stated that he had frequently been disturbed by a coffee shop in the street. As he went to 'reprimand one of the visitors to the coffee shop', his gun, 'accidentally went off'. (*Source:* Volkskrant)

17 October: In Den Bosch, a 17-year-old boy of Surinamese origin was raped and stabbed twelve times by a man of 22. The boy survived. His attacker had written several racist letters to the boy's family. Other inhabitants of Den Bosch had also received similar letters. In January 1987, the Judge declared the man to be of unsound mind. (*Source:* Telegraaf)

24 November: A 36-year-old man from Surinam was beaten up by two men, who told him that they 'dislike foreigners'. (*Source:* Telegraaf)

2 December: After regular telephone threats, the car of a vicar from Rotterdam was set on fire. The vicar helped refugees, the homeless and drug addicts. Two months earlier, swastikas had been painted on his car and stickers with 'Foreigners out' had been stuck to his house. (*Source:* Trouw)

Notes and documents

The far Right in Europe: a guide

AUSTRIA

Background

At the time of the Anschluss (annexation of Austria by Nazi Germany) in 1938, there was already a 500,000-strong Austrian Nazi Party, which drew its strength from the movements of anti-Semitism and pan-Germanism which had begun in the nineteenth century and accelerated after the First World War. Central to Austrian fascism in the post-war period has been the question of the Alto Adige (South Tyrol), which Austrian nationalists demand should be re-annexed from Italy. Traditionally, this area has been used as a base for right-wing terrorist activity. In the mid-1980s, a police estimate put the number of far-right activists at about 20,000. In 1986, former nazi, Kurt Waldheim, was elected president. An opinion survey carried out at the end of June 1988 showed that 47 per cent of those surveyed thought that National Socialism had brought as much good as bad to the country.

Far-right organisations

Freiheitliche Partei Osterreich (FPO)
Although affiliated to the Liberal International, the Freiheitliche Partei Österreich (FPO) stands on the far Right of Austrian politics, pursuing anti-foreigner policies, in general, and against the Slovene minority in Carinthia in particular. In 1989, the FPO won 29 per cent of the vote in the province and 10 per cent nationally. The FPO's leader, Jorg Haider, is now chief minister in the province. Haider has attended reunions of former SS members and has held meetings with French Front National leader Le Pen and the German Republikaner leader, Schonhuber. In parliamentary elections in October 1990, the FPO gained 16.6 per cent of the vote and increased its presence in the Austrian parliament from sixteen to thirty-three seats.

National Democratic Party (NPD)
This cultural organisation was formerly led by Dr Robert Burger, once convicted for terrorism in the South Tyrol region. He has also been the Director of the Commission for Truth in History which denies the Nazi genocide of the Jews.

Racial violence*

In 1985, nine neo-nazis were sent for trial for a series of attacks on Jewish-owned property.

BELGIUM

Background

In the 1960s, right-wing groups flourished and over a dozen organisations were formed to exploit discontent over Belgium's loss of the Congo. Jean Thiriat's 'Jeune Europe' linked up with the OAS, providing shelter for French terrorists.

Traditionally, fascist groups in Belgium have reflected the regional/ linguistic divide between the Flemish-, French- and German-speaking regions. During the Nazi period, groups like De Vlag (The Flag) demanded annexation to Germany and incorporation into the Third Reich. There were also collaborationist movements such as the Catholic 'Rexists' and the Vlaams National Verbond. According to a 1990 survey, 7 per cent of people in Brussels said they would vote for the French-oriented Parti Des Forces Nouvelles (PFN) and 8 per cent of the Flemish population for the Vlaams Blok (VB). Belgium is also the country which hosts the annual gathering of fascist organisations, which takes place at Diksmuide.

Far-right organisations

Vlaams Blok (VB)
The Flemish VB, founded in 1979, is the direct political descendant of the pre-war fascist movement. Some of its members were previously members of the *Vlaamse Militanten Order* (VMO), which was founded by wartime collaborators in 1949 and which was proscribed in the early 1980s as a result of its involvement in violence. VB's programme is one of Flemish nationalism and racism. It is opposed to the bilingual Belgian state and seeks the unification of the Flemish-speaking provinces with the Netherlands.

In 1986, the VB won two seats in the Belgian national parliament and now holds three. In municipal elections in autumn 1988, the VB trebled its 1982 vote, winning 17.7 per cent on an anti-immigrant and anti-foreigner platform in Antwerp, giving it ten seats in the city parliament and thirteen in the rest of Flanders. In the European parliament elections the following year, VB vice-president Karel

---

* The violence detailed in these sections is only an indicator of recent events and by no means exhaustive.

Dillen was elected with 20 per cent of the vote (214,000 votes) in the Flanders province, after a campaign around the slogan 'Our own people first'.

Front National (FN)
Founded in 1983 as a sister party to the French organisation of the same name, most of the FN's membership was reportedly drawn from the banned VMO. It is estimated to have about 1,000 members. It has two seats on the local council in Brussels city and one in Molenbeek, a suburb of Brussels. In September 1990, a civil servant who leaked an internal government document to the FN regarding refugees was dismissed.

Parti Des Forces Nouvelles (PFN)
The PFN is a smaller grouping formed in 1982. During the 1987 general election campaign, it distributed leaflets saying 'Halt the Barbarians', with cartoon drawings of Arabs. The PFN attempts to recruit among skinheads and football hooligans. In 1988, seven of its members were convicted of physical attacks on immigrants, although they were given only light sentences. In 1990, three fascists were arrested by police, accused of membership of a private army, *DARE*, linked to the PFN and the *Companions of Justice*. Another street-activist organisation encouraging racial violence is *L'Assaut*.

Racial violence

In 1987, a Burundese refugee was murdered by skinheads in Louvain. Members of the PFN have been associated with racist attacks. In October 1985, five PFN members, armed with steel bars, knives and an axe, attacked the home of a Moroccan family in Molenbeek.

DENMARK

Background

Text-books on the history of European fascism tend to have little to say on indigenous Danish far-right movements, citing instead Danish resistance to the German occupation of 1940-45. However, small indigenous fascist organisations such as the Danmarks Nasjonal-Sosjalistske Arbejder Parti (DNSP), founded in 1930, did exist prior to occupation, but were incorporated into the German Nazi Party under the Reich. The history of post-war fascist groups can be traced back to these Nazi forerunners; today racist violence is directed towards immigrants, principally Muslims, who are accused of destroying the cultural (and biological) integrity of the nation; of being the 'arsenic in pure Danish water'.

Far-right organisations

Dansk Nasjonal Sosjalistisk Bund (DNSB)
The DNSB was formed in the late 1960s as the Danish National Socialist Youth, and led by Poul Riis-Knudsen, head of the World Union of National Socialists. The DNSB, which claims 1,000 members, is the main fascist organisation in Denmark, is openly nazi and calls for the expulsion of immigrants and the sterilisation of non-Europeans residing in Denmark. In 1984, Riis-Knudsen caused controversy by using the state-owned radio to call for the deportation of immigrants on the grounds that 'race-mixing is threatening our biological heritage'.

Fremskridtpartiet (Progress Party)
The Fremskridtpartiet was formed in 1972 by its current leader, Mogens Glistrup. It promises to expel all Muslims and refugees. In the May 1988 elections, it doubled its proportion of the vote to 9 per cent. This gave it sixteen of the country's 179 parliamentary seats. The following year, the party won 235 seats in local elections, having held only thirty-five in the period 1985-9. In May 1988, the Copenhagen headquarters of the Socialist Workers Party (SAP) was firebombed by Danish fascists following a high profile campaign against the Progress Party and its leader.

Other groups
There is also a proliferation of smaller anti-immigrant organisations, like the *Citizens' List, Stop Immigration*, the *Danish Association* and the *Party of the Elderly*.

Racial violence

Racism has focussed mainly on Third World refugees, who form the main group of 'foreigners' in the country. There were violent attacks on refugees in Sjalland in 1985 and in Copenhagen and Blokhus the following year. Organisations and individuals who have supported refugees have been targeted in an organised campaign of harassment and intimidation by the DNSB, a campaign dubbed the 'Strategy of Silence' because of its purpose of silencing anti-racists. In October 1985, a Copenhagen taxi driver was found murdered after several anonymous calls had demanded that the government announce a halt to all immigration and the expulsion of immigrants. The callers, who identified themselves as 'Greenjackets' (racists and fascists who terrorise immigrants), threatened to kill taxi drivers and police officers if this demand was not met.

FRANCE

Background

From the 1920s to the 1940s France generated pseudo-fascist nationalist movements in profuse numbers, the most notorious of which was
Action Française. And from 1940 to 1944 the Vichy regime collaborated with the Nazis. Anti-Semitism grew and thousands of Jews were
deported. Almost immediately after the Second World War, right-
wing racist groups re-emerged, with the present Front National
leader, Jean Marie Le Pen, active among them from 1945 onwards. Le
Pen was elected to the National Assembly in 1956 for the Poujadists,
and again in 1958 for the Centre National des Independants et Paysans
(CNIP).

It was the Algerian war, in particular, that provided the occasion
for neo-fascists to regroup in the 1950s, now under the banner of the
Organisation de L'Armée Secrète (OAS). This was a period of intense
fascist activity.

In the 1970s, various fascist parties continued the tradition of
periodic large-scale street demonstrations, terrorist attacks and racial
violence. Only in the 1980s did the Front National emerge as the
principal far-right group, bringing electoral success and a national
political profile to racism.

Far-right organisations

Front National (FN)

Founded in 1972, its present leader, Jean Marie Le Pen, was a
paratrooper during the Algerian war. The FN has an estimated
membership of 100,000, but its support ranges widely throughout all
levels of French society. It produces a weekly newspaper, *National
Hebdo*. Both anti-Arab and anti-Semitic, it calls for the repatriation of
'immigrants', an end to the Islamification of France, and claims that
the gas chambers were a mere 'detail' of the Second World War.

Since its breakthrough in 1983, its electoral success has been
remarkable. There have, though, been some fluctuations; in 1986,
under proportional representation, it won thirty-five seats in the
national assembly; in 1988, in a two-round system, it captured only
one. The same year, Le Pen himself achieved a staggering 14.4 per
cent of the vote against Mitterrand in the first round of the presidential
elections. Since 1984, the FN has also held ten seats in the European
parliament and is the major party in the Technical Group of the
European Right. Its national and Europe-wide presence is backed up
by a strong, locally-based organisation. Through pacts with other
right-wing parties, it has managed to dominate many local councils,

gaining its first mayor in 1988. It currently has one deputy in the national assembly, ten MEPs and 842 local councillors. The effect of its election campaigns and local grassroots organisation has led, on the one hand, to a serious escalation in racial violence, and, on the other, to a sharp right-wing shift by all the major political parties on the race issue.

Parti National Français et Européen (PNFE)
A nazi street force, PNFE has links with other right-wing terrorist groups, especially in Italy. It is known to recruit amongst the skinhead followers of rock bands such as 'Legion 88', 'Front 242' and 'Bunker 84'.

Faisceaux Nationalistes Européens (FNE)
Formed in 1980, following the banning of the Fédération d'Action Nationale et Européenne (FANE) after a series of terrorist outrages, it is led by Marc Frederiksen and publishes *Notre Europe Combattante*.

Troisième Voie
Troisième Voie is active among skinhead gangs which attack black people and gays. It has a youth section called *Jeunesse Nationaliste Revolutionnaire* and publishes *Jeune Solidariste*. They are part of a growing network of Third Position fascists across Europe who, inspired by the works of the Italian fascist, Julius Evola, describe themselves as 'political soldiers'. Opposing 'both capitalism and communism', the Third Positionists aim to destabilise society and create a national revolution.

Racial violence

Of twenty 'foreigners' killed in the last four years, all but one were of North African origin. Particular concern has been expressed at the attitude of the police to acts of racism. An extreme right-wing police union, the FPIP, has the support of some 6.9 per cent of the police force.

Anti-Semitic attacks, such as the bombing in March 1985 of a Jewish film festival and the desecration of Jewish cemeteries, have also increased, as have arson attacks and bombings of 'immigrant' homes and meeting places, such as a bomb attack in March 1990 of a mosque at Rennes.

GERMANY

Background

Until 1987, when the extreme right German People's Union obtained more than the 5 per cent minimum needed to gain a seat in Bremen, no nazi party had won seats in West Germany at *Land* (state) or national levels since the National Demokratische Partei (NPD) in 1966-8. There have been numerous small neo-nazi groupings in the post-war period and a fear that ex-nazis have simply remained dormant, finding their way into the ministries or police force.

According to official statistics, membership of nazi organisations had fallen from 76,000 in 1954 to 23,000 in 1985. In 1988, however, the *Verfassungschutz* (the West German secret service) estimated that the number of activists had risen to 28,000. Of the twenty neo-nazi groups recognised, the Deutsche Volksunion (DVU) was then the largest with 12,000 members.

Far-right organisations

Republikaner (REP)

The REP was founded in 1983 by dissidents from Franz Josef Strauss' Christian Social Union when Strauss was considered to be getting too sympathetic to the Communist regime in East Germany. Those creating the new party included journalist Franz Schonhuber, a former Waffen-SS officer, who eventually became the party's leader. The party, however, has always denied that it is nazi.

The REP, which calls for the repatriation of foreign workers, won 3 per cent of the vote in the Bavarian state parliament election in 1986, but its major breakthrough came in January 1989, when it obtained 7.5 per cent (94,000 votes) in elections to the West Berlin house of representatives and won eleven seats. In the 1989 European parliament elections, it won 7.1 per cent, giving it six seats. (The Republikaner obtained 2 million of the 2.65 million votes cast for the four racist parties putting up candidates.) In October, the Republikaner won 8.5 per cent of the vote in the North Rhine-Westphalia *Land* elections, obtaining seats in Cologne, Dusseldorf and Bonn. Later the same year, it won 9.6 per cent of the vote in Stuttgart and 9.8 in Mannheim.

As a party for which German unification was a prime aim, the Republikaner seemed to lose support as the Berlin wall came down and German unity became a real possibility. In 1990, its share of the vote declined significantly, although it still managed to obtain 3.3 per cent in elections to the Saarland parliament and 5.4 per cent in municipal elections in Bavaria. In December 1990 it won less than the 5 per cent needed to take up seats in parliament.

National Democratic Party (NPD)
Like the Republikaner, the NPD has done well in local elections by exploiting racism. In 1989, it secured 6.6 per cent of the vote in Hesse and seven seats in Frankfurt. In Tuttlingen, where the Republikaners did not stand, the NPD won 9.3 per cent of the votes for the city parliament elections.

Both the Republikaner and the NPD have been active in East Germany. In 1989, soon after the Berlin wall was breached, the Red Army memorial in East Berlin was daubed with fascist slogans, as were Soviet war graves in the city. On New Year's Eve, neo-nazi skinheads ran riot in Gera. In Dresden and Gorlitz, near the Polish border, 'Hitler lives' and swastikas were daubed on public buildings. Republikaner and NPD material from West Germany has been circulated widely and, in February 1990, anti-fascists reported seeing 400 neo-nazis active around the 20,000-strong march for German unity. A speaker from the platform represented a new neo-nazi organisation, the *National Democrats of Central Germany*.

Other groups
Other far-right groups include the *Free German Workers Party* (FAP) (traditional nazi) and the *Nationalistiche Front* (NF). The NF strategy is identified with the Third Position. One member, Josef Saller, was recently jailed for twelve years for setting fire to a Turkish home, killing four people.

Racial violence

Alongside these electoral successes has come an upsurge in popular racism towards migrants, particularly Turks and other non-Europeans. In 1989, a Turkish youth was murdered in an apparently racially-motivated attack in Berlin and four people were killed in a racist arson attack in Schwandorf, Bavaria. The youth responsible was reported to have carried out the arson attack on the home of a Turkish family because he hated foreigners. After West Germany's world cup victory in July 1990, foreigners were attacked in several cities. Neo-nazi computer games circulate, encouraging racism, fascism and militarism. These include 'The Aryan Test', produced by 'Adolf Hitler Software Ltd', and an 'Anti-Turkish Test'.

In May 1990, in East Germany, a Jewish cemetery in East Berlin was desecrated and the graves of Bertolt Brecht and his wife, Helene Wiegel, were daubed with the words 'Jewish pigs'. In June, 200 East German skinheads formed a human swastika around the Marx-Engels memorial in East Berlin. Nor have attacks been confined to property. Mozambican and Vietnamese workers, in particular, have become the object of attack. In 1990, a young man was seriously injured in East

Berlin after a petrol bomb thrown by nazis attacking a multi-national centre exploded in his face. In May, Mozambicans were attacked by gangs with stones, knives and bottles. Attempts were made to storm their hostel and the Mozambicans were forced to barricade themselves in the building. In another attack, a Mozambican was beaten and had to be hospitalised. Again, the residence of Mozambican workers was put under siege. According to a report in *Caribbean Times* (4 September 1990), because of the levels of violence, blacks could only move around in groups, even during the day; at night, they had to stay indoors. In August, six people were injured after a crowd of Germans stoned a hostel housing Mozambican workers in Treppin. In Leipzig, foreign students spoke of their fear of growing racism after an anti-fascist cafe was fire-bombed.

GREECE

Background

Greek fascism was based traditionally on anti-communism. 'The government of the Greek colonels' was established after a coup in 1967, led by George Papadopoulos and Stylianos Pattakos. Largely described as fascist, the evidence of the regime's methods of torture and brutality led the Dutch and Swedish governments to arraign Greece before the European Court of Human Rights. The armed forces relinquished power in 1974.

Far-right organisations

Greek National Political Society (EPEN)
Formed in 1984 as the organisation of the imprisoned former dictator Papadopoulos, EPEN won one of Greece's twenty-four European parliament seats the same year, but secured less than 1 per cent of the vote in national elections the following year. The party lost its one seat in the European parliament in 1988, and in national elections in 1990 again won less than 1 per cent of the vote. According to the 1990 European parliament report, a number of smaller far-right groups have engaged in attacks on Jews, gypsies and Muslims and, during the period of Socialist Party government, in acts of economic sabotage.

ITALY

Background

After the Second World War, several small 'nostalgic' fascist organisations were formed. Based principally on anti-communism, they attacked left organisations and gave their antics names like 'Black Bear', 'Camel' or 'Scorpion'. In 1946, the Movimento Sociale Italiano (MSI) was formed in Rome, claiming it was inspired by the 'revolutionary fascism of 1919.' Later, several terrorist organisations emerged, like the Third Positionist Nuclei Armati Rivoluzionari (NAR), which in August 1980 bombed Bologna railway station, killing eighty-six people.

Far-right organisations

Movimento Sociale Italiano (MSI)
The largest and most important fascist party in Italy is the Movimento Sociale Italiano – Destra Nazionale, usually known as the MSI, which was founded in 1946 by second level leaders of the fascist regime and of the Italian Social Republic, from which it derived its name. For most of its life it was led by Giorgio Almirante, a former minister in the Mussolini regime. (When he died in 1988, some 10,000 people marched at his funeral.) The MSI's electoral fortunes peaked in 1972, when it obtained 8.7 per cent of the votes (2.9 million) in elections to the chamber of deputies. By 1987, the MSI's share of the vote had fallen to 5.9 per cent (2.3 million votes). Nevertheless, in the 1989 European parliament elections, the MSI still won four seats with 5.6 per cent of the votes, one less than it had held previously. In the same year, the MSI became the majority right-wing party in the South Tyrol. In elections in the provincial capital Bolzano, it won 27 per cent of the vote.

Connections have been made between the MSI and right-wing terrorists. An MSI member, Giuseppe Misso, was alleged by Italian police to have taken part in the bombing of the Naples-Milan train in 1984, in which fifteen people were killed, as was Massimo Abbatangelo, recently elected an MSI member of the Italian parliament. Many of those involved in terrorist groups, such as *Ordine Nuovo* (New Order) and the *Nuclei Armati Rivoluzionari* (NAR), were originally members of the MSI.

Lombard League
The Lombard League is a separatist organisation that believes that there should be a federal Italy of separate republics – north, central and south. In the European parliament elections in 1989 the League, which denies it is fascist, polled 8 per cent of the vote in Lombardy, and 1.8 per cent overall, enough to give it one member. The League's share of the vote increased to 20 per cent in local elections in May 1990. Recent polls give the League 29 per cent of the votes in the region. The League has also recently filed for a national referendum opposing

government plans to grant the right of abode to immigrants resident in the country. The Italian Football Federation has accused the League of 'fomenting racism on the terraces'.

Racial violence

In the summer of 1989, the town council of Villa Literno, a small town north of Naples, put forward plans to build a centre to house 130 African seasonal workers. This was greeted by a petition which secured vast local support to ban black people from the town altogether. A few weeks later, a South African refugee, Jerry Essan Masslo, was killed in Villa Literno. 200,000 people marched in Rome in October in protest. Also in 1989, a southern Italian migrant was beaten to death in Verona. The following year, four African street-vendors in Florence narrowly escaped death when a fire-bomb gutted the caravan in which they were sleeping. In Milan, one man was burned to death and scores injured in a fire which swept through a block of flats inhabited by immigrants. In Padua, police investigated letters circulated by the 'Veneto Ku Klux Klan', urging the killing of blacks who refused to go home.

NETHERLANDS

Background

Invaded by Germany in 1940, the only indigenous fascist group of any note was Anton Mussert's Nationaal-Socialistische Beweging, which garnered 4 per cent of the Dutch vote in the 1937 elections. Mussert's collaborationists supplied Hitler's armed forces with a larger number of volunteers, in proportion to the population, than any other European country.

Far-right organisations

Centrum Partij and Centrum Demokraten
The extreme right Centrum Partij (CP) was formed in 1980, partly by ex-members of the openly nazi *Nederlandse Volksunie* (Union of the Dutch People). In a bid to gain greater popular support, the CP took up the question of immigration as one of its main issues, using the slogan, '500,000 foreigners in our country and 500,000 unemployed'. In 1986, the CP became the Centrum Demokraten (CD), with the breaking away of the splinter *Centrum Partij '86*. Although it has just over 1,000 members, its leader, Hans Jaanmat, was elected to the second chamber of the national parliament in 1989 with over 80,000

votes. In 1990, the CD, together with the Centrum Partij '86, increased their local representation from two to fifteen council seats, mainly in Rotterdam, where they took 7.1 per cent of the votes, Amsterdam (6.8 per cent) and The Hague (6.4 per cent).

Other groups
Other far-right groups include the *Young Front Netherlands*, whose leader, Stewart Mordaunt, claims that 'national socialism is the only way to preserve Western Europe' and the *Action Front of National Socialists*, which has had some success in recent local elections.

Racial violence

The 1985 European parliament committee of inquiry noted that, compared to countries such as Germany, France and the UK, racism and discrimination in the Netherlands took on a less aggressive form. The Anne Frank Foundation, however, has documented numerous cases of racially-motivated attacks against foreigners, including the murder of a 15-year-old Antillean, Kerwin Duynmeyer, by a Dutch youth in August 1984. The Amsterdam municipality's race unit noted a 200 per cent increase in complaints between April 1985 and April 1986. In 1986, complaints of abuse by the police increased by 50 per cent. In 1986, a cafe in Schiedam frequented by immigrants was bombed.

NORWAY

Background

Norway was occupied in the Second World War by the Germans who set up a puppet government under Quisling. Nationalist opposition to the occupation, however, has not led to a sustained anti-fascist/anti-racist tradition. Whilst overt neo-nazi groups have remained small, anti-immigration racist movements have grown rapidly in recent years. This culminated in a large vote (13.7 per cent) for the anti-immigration Progress Party in the 1989 elections.

Far-right organisations

Fremskrittspartiet (Progress Party)
Founded in 1973, the Progress Party campaigns on the issues of tax reform and stronger immigration controls. In the 1987 local elections, it gained 12 per cent of the vote and in 1989 it increased its share of the 165 seats in the national parliament (the *Storting*) from two to twenty-two. This makes it the third largest party in parliament, and,

under its leader Carl Hargen, it holds the balance of power.

People's Movement against Immigration (FMI)
Reputedly the largest extra-parliamentary far-right group campaigning on immigration, the leader of the FMI, Arne Myrdal, was recently imprisoned for a year for organising a plot to bomb a camp for refugees in Arendal. In June 1990, the FMI organised an anti-immigration march in Arendal, the first of its kind since the Second World War.

Nationalists (Nasjonalisten)
The Nasjonalisten sees itself as the successor to the Norsk Front which was active in the 1970s. Its leader, Eric Blucher, has had contact with other far-right groups in Europe, including the National Front in Britain. He has also attended the international fascist rally at Diksmuide, Belgium.

National People's Party (Nasjonalt Folkeparti – NF)
The NF co-publishes, with other Scandinavian nazi groups, *Nordic Order*. Jan Oegärd, its leader, was imprisoned in 1984 for incitement to racial hatred and was one of eleven NF members arrested in 1985 in connection with the bombing of a mosque in Oslo.

Other anti-immigration groups
Several smaller racist organisations have recently been formed. These include the *National Democrats* in early 1990 and the *Home Country Party* (taking its name from the Norwegian wartime resistance), both break-away groups from the *Stop Immigration Party*.

Racial violence

There was a four-fold increase in racial attacks between 1987 and 1989. Shops and houses have been set on fire, and attacks have included the use of guns and bombs. There have been a number of murders. In summer 1989, a man convicted of conspiracy to dynamite a hostel for refugees had his sentence deferred by the court to enable him to campaign for the anti-immigrant Progress Party. In May 1989, a bomb went off in the Red Cross refugee centre at Eidsvoll. Forty-nine African asylum-seekers were in the centre at the time; fortunately no one was killed.

PORTUGAL

Background

In the post-war period, the powers of the armed security forces grew under Salazar's authoritarian regime, which displayed many similarities to the corporatism of Italian fascism. The leading functionaries of the secret police (the PIDE), formed in 1940, had, for instance, been trained by Gestapo agents. The Legiao Portuguesa, formed in 1936, was modelled on the German SA and the Italian fascist militia. The authoritarianism and racism of the Salazar regime came to the fore over its handling of Portugal's colonial possessions in Africa. In 1961, at the start of the revolutionary uprising in Angola, some 50,000 PIDE reinforcements were sent in. A medical officer, giving evidence to a special committee of the United Nations, spoke out against the extreme butchery of the Portugese: 'People who had been arrested were unloaded from trucks as if they were logs. If a soldier wanted to, he was allowed to select "his victim" and kill him on the spot. The hands of the dead were cut off in order to spread terror among the living. The machete served as a guillotine.'

Far-right organisations

Circulo Europeo de Amigos de Europea (CEDADE) – Portugal
There are a number of relatively small fascist groupings active in Portugal. The most important is probably the youth-oriented CEDADE-Portugal (European Circle of Friends of Europe), formed in 1980 as an offshoot of the Spanish CEDADE. Openly nazi, it is strongest in Oporto, but acts as a focus for cooperation with smaller groups.

Movimento Accao Nacional (National Action Movement)
The MAN has links with other European nazi groups, including the British National Front and the Belgian PFN.

Racial violence

Skinhead violence against the country's African inhabitants led to the creation in early 1990 of a government committee to monitor and study the situation of minorities in Portugal. In October 1989, neo-nazi skinheads murdered Jose da Carvalho, leader of the Portuguese Revolutionary Socialist Party, and injured several others.

SPAIN

Background

General Franco's Nationalist forces were supported during the Spanish civil war (1936-9) by Italy and Germany. During the war years, Franco had led the Spanish fascist party, the Falange, which he later tried to distance himself from. He remained head of state until 1975. Virulently anti-communist, the Franquist system is said to have most resembled Italian fascism.

Far-right organisations

The 'Nostalgists'
Several right-wing organisations, like the *Frente Nacional* and *Solidaridad Española*, nostalgic for the Franco dictatorship, have emerged recently – as has the *Falange Española*.

Circulo Español de Amigos de Europa (Spanish Circle of Friends of Europe)
CEDADE was formed in 1965 and has approximately thirty offices in Spain. It has forged links with racist groups in Europe and voiced support for the Catalan independence movement through literature stating: 'We are Catalans, therefore we are racist.'

Racial violence

Black workers from Africa and gypsies, in particular, are the object of violence. In July 1986, more than thirty gypsy families in Andalusia had to flee to a nearby village after their homes were burnt down. Refused accommodation there, they were eventually provided with tents by the Spanish Red Cross under the protection of the civil guard. Three months later, in the town of Ciudad Real, another group of gypsies had to flee an arson attack. Attacks on black workers include: a Guinean worker who, in May 1989, had his hands broken in a bar in Almeria; and a Moroccan worker who was beaten to death by two Spaniards in a fight.

SWEDEN

Background

Despite the growth of indigenous fascist parties in the 1930s, no strong fascist organisation developed in the post-war period. Fascist groups such as the Malmö-Brown International (founded 1951) were small

and largely irrelevant. However, a breakthrough for the far Right
came in 1980 with the formation of the Keep Sweden Swedish (BSS)
party (now defunct). Since then, far-right organisations have split and
regrouped. These small groupings are increasingly drawing inspiration from fascist organisations across Europe.

Far-right organisations

Sweden Democrats
This was formed in 1988 when it split from the *Sweden Party* (which
has since remained largely inactive). By far the largest far-right group,
its membership is estimated to be 2,000. The group campaigns on the
issue of immigration. When it stood in the 1988 elections, it gained
1,100 votes, a surprisingly large share, considering it had just split with
the Sweden Party. In fact, this vote was the largest post-war vote for a
racist party in Sweden.

Nordiska Rikspartiet
Formed in 1956, the party has less than 500 members. Its youth wing,
Reichpartie Action Group, is notorious for its involvement in racial
violence.

Europeiska Arbetarpartiet
This small right group gained notoriety following the murder of Prime
Minister Olof Palme, when one suspect was discovered to have links
with the group. It is the Swedish branch of the European Labour
Committee, headed by Lyndon LaRouche's National Democratic
Policy Committee (United States). It receives on average 100-200
votes in elections.

Skanepartiet (Skane Party)
This right-wing populist party is based in Skane in southern Sweden.
In 1985, it won a surprising 7.4 per cent of the votes in the municipal
elections in Malmö, gaining six seats in the local parliament and
causing the first defeat for the Social Democrats for seventy years.
Until the Social Democrats won back Malmö in 1988, this racist party
was frequently sought as a coalition partner by the conservative ruling
coalition to gain a majority.

Racial violence

Throughout 1990, there has been a wave of arson and other attacks on
refugee centres. These include: a series of attacks in the summer in
Mariestad by racist youth, including an arson attack on a refugee
centre; three attacks on refugee centres between 26-27 May 1990, in

which eleven people were injured. (In January 1989, it was reported that about ten warders who work in the Kronoberg remand centre in Stockholm, where asylum-seekers are detained, belonged to racist associations such as the BSS (Keep Sweden Swedish).)

Before that, in the summer of 1989, there had been reports of racist attacks and fights between Swedish and 'immigrant' youths in several towns and regions of Sweden, including Eskilstuna, Lesjöfors, Overum, Jokoping, Aneby and Jamtland.

SWITZERLAND

Background

The far Right in Switzerland has traditionally drawn succour from a conservatism that sees the presence of 'foreigners' as a threat to the Swiss way of life. Despite neutrality in the Second World War, indigenous fascist organisations such as the National Front attempted to pressurise the government to halt the flow of Jewish refugees, encouraging the growth of anti-Semitism. In the post-war period, prejudice was directed towards foreign workers, principally from southern Europe, who were drawn to the country to do the dirty, manual jobs. The foreign worker problem 'is the highly sensitive detonator which can set off the charge of Swiss nationalism', reported the *Sonntags Journal* in 1970. In that year, right-wing MP James Schwarzenbach (who has been compared to Britain's Enoch Powell) forced a referendum to demand that foreign residents in any one canton should not exceed 10 per cent of the total population. Today, the racism of small far-right organisations, drawing on the anti-Semitic and anti-foreigner strands in Swiss society, is directed principally against the new asylum-seekers, the refugees of the Third World.

Far-right organisations

Nationale Aktion fur Volk und Heimat (National Action for People and Homeland)
The National Action for People and Homeland has been the leading party on Switzerland's far Right since it was formed in 1961. During the 1970s, it had sufficient support to force the holding of three referenda on ending immigration, and in 1985 secured 15 per cent of the vote in Berne, Geneva and Zurich. Since then, however, there have been numerous splits on the far Right and its influence has waned.

Other groups
In 1985, an overtly nazi grouping was formed, the *National*

Sozialistische Partei/Parti National Socialiste. The following year, a former leader of Nationale Aktion, Valentin Oehen, formed the *Liberal Ecologist Party*, claiming that hardliners had given the party a simplistic, racist and extremist image. The *Patriotic Front* and *La Section Democratique Suisse* are two other splinter groups, particularly vocal on refugee issues.

Racial violence

Members of the Patriotic Front (FP) and La Section Democratique Suisse have been involved in anti-Semitic attacks and racial violence. In 1990, six FP supporters were jailed after participating in raids between 1987 and 1989 on reception centres for asylum-seekers in the cantons of Zug and Uri.

Attacks on refugees, asylum-seekers and other foreigners have escalated in recent years. In 1989, four Tamil refugees died after an arson attack in Graubunden. In November 1989, a gang of thirty members of the far-right *Patriotische Burgerfront* attacked a refugee hostel in Zug, and in December several people were injured in an attack on a Zurich migrants' home. In early 1990, a 44-year-old Kurd was beaten to death in Freiburg. He and a friend had been pursued by a gang of youths armed with baseball bats. The killers had no known connection with any racist group, but the 'National Coordination' umbrella group of racists and fascists was reported to have been whipping up racial hatred in the area. In Rorschach, an area in which Patriotische Burgerfront has been active, three Tamils were shot at, and one wounded, as they walked home from work. Jewish cemeteries in St Gallen were desecrated in July 1990 and headstones daubed with the slogans 'Death to the Jews' and 'Heil Hitler'.

UNITED KINGDOM

Background

After the Second World War, Sir Oswald Mosley, who had previously modelled his British Union of Fascists on Italian fascism, attempted to revive fascism under the Union Movement. In the post-war period, there have been numerous fascist groupings, many of which have split off one from the other. Their programmes have been based on anti-black racism (in particular, calls for enforced repatriation), anti-Semitism and nostalgia for the British Empire. Other strands include support for Protestant paramilitary groups in Northern Ireland and opposition to British membership of the EC.

In the 1970s, the fascist groups, notorious for their racial violence,

bid for respectability by standing in local elections. Their greatest
success came in the Greater London Council elections of 1977, when
the National Front gained 200,000 votes. Since then, they have
declined as an electoral force.

Far-right organisations

National Front
Originally formed in 1967, its publications include, since 1986, *The
Flag*, *Vanguard* and *Lionheart*. The National Front (NF) has an
estimated membership of 500 and claims to be a party of the working
class. It seems increasingly to be influenced by 'Strasserism' – that is,
the ideology of the Strasser brothers, whose followers formed the
backbone of the SA brownshirts and who accused Hitler of betraying
the principles of National Socialism.

British National Party (BNP)
Formed in 1982 when it split off from the NF, its publications include
British Nationalist and *Spearhead*. The BNP has an estimated membership of 800 and is considered to be the most openly nazi of the
fascist groups in Britain. Its leader, John Tyndall, has been active
since the 1950s and is probably the most well-known fascist leader in
Britain. He has been imprisoned for both paramilitary activities and
inciting racial hatred.

The BNP has been particularly active in the East End of London
where it has stood in local elections and organised a 'Rights for
Whites' march. It has also been very active in Scotland where there is a
high incidence of racial violence. In its campaigns, it argues that
whites, not blacks, are the real victims of race attacks.

Third Way
The comparatively insignificant Third Way was formed in 1990 out of
the rump of the NF that remained after the split with the Flag group in
1986. Its esoteric magazine, *Third Way*, argues for Third Position
politics on a range of topics, including the environment and ethnic
separatism.

Blood and Honour
The youth-cult organisation Blood and Honour produces a magazine
of the same name and has a following largely among skinheads in
Britain and Europe. The most well-known of the fascist music bands is
'Screwdriver', whose lead singer is Ian Stuart. Blood and Honour has
remained relatively quiet since an international music gig organised in
London in May 1990 was sabotaged by the anti-fascist movement,
which also forced it to shut down its retails outlets in Carnaby Street in
central London.

Racial violence

Since the 1970s, there have been approximately sixty deaths of black people resulting from acts of racial violence.

In January 1989, a Somalian refugee was killed by a white gang in Edinburgh; in July 1989 a 14-year-old boy was killed after being hit in the neck by an air-pistol pellet in Oldham; in September 1989, an Asian man had a heart attack after being attacked on a bus between Rotherham and Sheffield; in November 1989, an Asian taxi driver was stabbed to death in Southall, London and, most recently, a 17-year-old schoolboy was stabbed in Bradford in what is believed to be a racial incident.

General incidents of racial harassment against black people are estimated at 70,000 per year. A recent wave of anti-Semitic attacks has included attacks on Jewish property and the desecration of Jewish cemeteries.

Compiled by the Campaign Against Racism and Fascism from the following sources:

Searchlight
Migration Newssheet
Committee of Inquiry into the Rise of Racism and Fascism in Europe, *Report on the Findings of the Inquiry* (European Parliament, 1985).
Committee of Inquiry into Racism and Xenophobia, *Report* (European Parliament, 1990).
Geoffrey Harris, *The Dark Side of Europe: the extreme right today* (Edinburgh University Press, 1990).
Klaus von Beyme (ed.), *Right-wing Extremism in Western Europe* (Frank Cass, 1988).
Ciaran O Maolain, *The Radical Right: a world directory* (Longman, 1987).
Angelo del Boca and Mario Giovana, *Fascism Today* (Heinemann, 1970).
Together with articles from the national press, and a number of magazines.

Report of the European Committee on racism and xenophobia: a critique*

When one considers the kind of opposition that this report has generated within the European parliament – not amongst the 'Group of the European Right', but amongst Socialist and Liberal MEPS** – then the fact that it was completed at all is itself remarkable. Where one would be wrong, however, would be to associate the refusal of MEPs to back the report's key recommendations with anything inherently radical in the committee's approach.

In fact, the findings of an initial inquiry into the rise of racism and fascism in Europe had already been published in 1985, leading to the adoption by the European parliament of a Joint Declaration Against Racism and Xenophobia. Many MEPs, however, decided that it was necessary to update the material, and produce a more comprehensive report. Accordingly, a committee of Euro MPs was selected and held thirteen meetings between 23 November 1989 and 17 July 1990. The committee invited written submissions and held two hearings – one where the views of national civil servants were garnered, the other to gather evidence from groups deemed to have some experience of monitoring racism and fascism.

What the committee does deserve credit for is bringing together previously scattered information on extreme right-wing activity throughout Europe. In several European countries, there are now national fascist parties represented in parliaments and on local councils. A part of the electoral strategy of such parties – and, indeed, of other right-wing groupings like Italy's *Lombard League* – is the exploitation of long-festering European ethnic, regional and linguistic divides. Then there is the growth of youth cults, principally around music and football, the members of which provide the footsoldiers for more organised fascist groupings. Such racial terrorism finds its complement in popular racism (particularly anti-Arab racism) and the growth of a virulent anti-immigrant and anti-refugee lobby. Finally (particularly in Eastern Europe where communism no longer

---

* *Report of the Committee of Inquiry into Racism and Xenophobia*. Rapporteur: Mr Glyn Ford (Brussels, European Parliament Sessions Document, 1989).
** French Liberals were hostile to the committee's proposal to allow voting rights in local elections to migrants with five years' residence. The Socialist Group in the European parliament then condemned their stance, attacking the French Liberal leader Giscard d'Estaing. At which point, French Socialist MEPs took fright, threatening to invoke the 'conscience clause', defy group policy and vote against the report. Hence, in order that the report be produced at all, the committee had to agree to a compromise whereby the European Commission was asked to 'study seriously' the report's recommendations, rather than 'endorse' them as would previously have been the case.[1] In the event, voting was close: 188 for, 146 against.

ideologically coheres the nation), there is the horrifying resurgence of anti-Semitism. The violent activities of organisations like Russia's *Pamyat* are fuelled by the theories of the 'Historical Revisionists', who deny that the gas chambers ever existed or that six million Jews died in the Nazi Holocaust.

But, having assiduously listed the facts, the committee failed to draw the conclusions that demanded to be made precisely because it would then need to look at racism in the economic and political context of each country (and make recommendations accordingly). Hobbled by its remit from doing this,* the committee settled for the soft option of the cultural/psychological view of racism.

Basically, there are two ways of studying the present resurgence in fascist and right-wing activity: either you situate it within the framework of the European body politic as a whole, examine the health of the whole organism, so to speak, or you see the growth of right-wing organisations as confined to the extremities of society, rather like a gangrenous limb that needs amputation. Either you relate racial prejudice to institutionalised racism, racist attacks to the imprimatur that the state gives to racism, or you examine prejudice in isolation, as a human failing, linking the growth in racist activity to a frightening (and, indeed, if you follow this line of reasoning, somewhat fatalistic) increase in xenophobia.

The report broadly follows the second approach. Hence its recommendations are geared towards either measuring prejudice through opinion polls (grandly called the 'European barometer') or studying it (through a special scientific investigation into the rise of xenophobia); towards providing cultural palliatives (like the 1985 Year of Racial Harmony) or penalising xenophobic behaviour (through a new European ombudsman). But anything less modest did not go unchallenged. For example, the demand for 'voting rights in local elections for immigrants with five years' residence' – a demand that many Socialist parties throughout Europe once adhered to before they realised it was an electoral liability – led some Socialists and Liberals in the European parliament to threaten to veto the report. And, because the committee members were loth to make judgements over each country's (racist) immigration policy, some of their key recommendations become rather double-edged. For example, they recommend that 'immigrants' with residential rights in one country should be issued with a European Resident's Card which would enable them to move

---

* It was obvious, too, that any report which did link the rise of racism with national and governmental policy would never get past the European Commission for further action. For the European Commission, which had requested the Runnymede Trust to do a 'comparative study into the ten member states' had quickly ditched that research after the initial report pointed to 'institutionalised discrimination', on the grounds that it was 'unwilling to enter into conflict with Member States'.

to member countries to find work. But since all 'immigrants', 'foreigners', 'blacks' invariably 'carry their passports on their faces',[2] the committee's distinction between 'legal' and 'illegal' is of comfort to neither.

What the recommendations really point to is the creation of an embryonic race relations structure within Europe to manage racial prejudice. 'If we can harmonise lawn-mower noise,' stated Glyn Ford, 'surely we can harmonise something as important as race relations.' Hence, Britain's Commission for Racial Equality, which is noted only for the failure of its objective, is held out as the model of 'an anti-racist institution' and France's SOS Racisme, which is as political as its slogan 'Don't touch my pal', the type of anti-racist movement that impresses national governments. There is a proposal for a 'European Migrants Forum for representative organisations from EC nations' but, given the lack of any genuine commitment to migrant and refugee communities, such a forum will only lead to a further augmentation of Europe's race relations structure and add a new layer of discredited 'immigrant leaders' to police Europe's bantustans.

Since even the more 'liberal' intentions of Euro MPs were thwarted by politicians who would brook no criticism of their national governments, or consider even limited change to the status quo, people like Le Pen could sit silently by as the debate about the committee's findings progressed, and see that their task was done. The attempts of some Socialists and Liberals, in particular, to disassociate themselves from the report were a genuine tribute to the influence right-wing and fascist ideologies are having on the European body politic. But, if the uprisings in Lyon are anything to go by, it is to the political struggles of black settlers, immigrant and refugee communities, that we must look to wipe the smile off Mr Le Pen's face.

Institute of Race Relations   LIZ FEKETE

References

1   See *New Statesman and Society* (19 October 1990).
2   A. Sivanandan, quoted in *Voice* (No. 407, 7 August 1990).

A note on *Ausländerfeindlichkeit*

In West Germany the term 'racism' is not used where discrimination, exclusionary practices and racialisation of people of non-German origin are concerned. Instead, one speaks of '*Ausländerfeindlichkeit*' – 'hostility against foreigners'. We feel it is necessary to analyse the terms in which reality is constructed: selecting certain concepts and abolishing others is a decision about what kind of reality one can take into account and what is concealed. As the term 'racism' is virtually taboo in political and theoretical discussions in Germany, the reality for which it stands is taboo as well. It is excluded from public discussions of today's conflicts. And the reasons why racism is taboo have much to do with recent German history, with German fascism. Much research has been done by the Left on capital's support for Hitler, and the Frankfurt School developed the concept of the 'authoritarian personality' to explain how individuals were led to support anti-Semitism. Yet, in public discussion generally, the question of why Hitler was supported by the vast majority of the German population is hardly ever asked.

In public political debate, there are two main ways of dealing with the past. The first (practised by the majority) is simply to suppress the memory of it. The second does recall the past, commemorates specific happenings, etc. But it conceptualises German fascism as something one cannot understand rationally; as the work of a few maniacs around Hitler. Both strategies, however, have the same effect in terms of our ideological approach to the present. According to dominant ideology, the Federal Republic of Germany (FRG) had nothing to do with the so-called Third Reich. This way of getting rid of the past, of its trauma, cannot be thought of simply as a sophisticated, socio-psychological means of suppressing reality. It is also a somewhat crude mechanism to re-establish and stabilise elements of the old power-structure under the pretence of establishing something entirely new. Everyone knows (everyone who wants to know, that is) that leading Nazis from all fields of society (judges, doctors, politicians) were given high positions in the 'new state'. This was possible because, under the new regime, they were not the same people any more – they had been reborn, rebaptised.

Now we can see why racism was not considered to exist in the FRG: racism and nationalism were the main ideologies of the fascist period. If they existed today, then something of that past would have survived. This becomes clearer if one examines the arguments used against those who insist on discussing racism.

We cannot speak of racism, it is said, because this would trivialise the suffering of the Jewish people during German fascism. Although such an argument seems to consider history instead of suppressing it, in fact it turns the racism of the Nazi-period into something so extraordinary, so aberrant, that it could never be repeated, ideologically or otherwise, except among neo-Nazi groups. But although we are far from saying that the organised killing of millions of people is identical with the forms of racism experienced today, we would, nevertheless, argue that to construct that racism of the past (which took the form of anti-Semitism) as something absolutely different from the ideologies and experiences of today means avoiding deeper analysis of racism in its current, as well as in its earlier forms. It is a way of avoiding the fact that these forms of racism were supported and carried out by millions of ordinary citizens. To admit this would mean accepting that those tendencies may not have simply disappeared, but are the very basis from which present forms of racism grow. To admit that fascism and anti-Semitism were supported by normal people would also mean realising that new, but equally cruel and brutal, forms of racism could arise again and be supported by millions of ordinary citizens.

It is said that in Germany we cannot speak about racism because foreigners are not of different races as are, for instance, black people in Britain. But this implies that there is scientific validity to the notion of different races and that the differences between 'races' can be judged by skin colour. So, on the one hand, this argument is still articulated within a racist ideology, while, on the other, it ignores the German past completely. For it was claimed that Jews were of a different race, although they had the same skin colour and looked no different from other Germans. Although a whole pseudo-science was invented to measure those pretended physical differences, a yellow star had to be used to make the 'difference' 'visible'. If one cannot speak about racism because it would undermine the dominant ideology of the 'new state', how does one conceptualise present conflicts? Here the term *Ausländerfeindlichkeit* is introduced. It allows us to speak about the present whilst avoiding the analysis of recent history.

Ausländerfeindlichkeit has been described by Hoffman and Even in *Soziologie der Ausländerfeindlichkeit* (Frankfurt, 1984) as 'every way in which foreigners are denied equal rights if they don't assimilate to German identity'. In their view, this denial originates in the 'concept of society' that Germans hold to. Germany is thought of as a homogeneous, purely German nation which does not include 'foreigners'. This means that either the concept has to be changed to correspond to the reality of a multicultural German society, or the reality has to be changed – that is, 'foreigners' have to be 'repatriated'. It is the latter option which is favoured by a large proportion of the German population and it is this which, according to Hoffman and Even, is the origin of *Ausländerfeindlichkeit*. Other theories, which rely more on an economic analysis, believe that *Ausländerfeindlichkeit* arises during economic crises when people are afraid of losing their jobs and are looking for scapegoats. Others claim that the state's policies on immigration cause *Ausländerfeindlichkeit* because, being mainly concerned with cutting down on and keeping out 'foreigners', they stigmatise people from other countries as a threat to German culture. People, it is said, repeat the anxieties and fears voiced by politicians and government.

These explanations do grasp some of the features of racism. But none of them inquires into the historical foundation of present-day *Ausländerfeindlichkeit*. None asks how do people come to be considered as 'foreigners'? This may seem obvious, but it is not. For instance, if we ask people to say what the term 'foreigner' conveys to them, they mention dark hair, different religions, different ways of dress, etc. Northern Europeans, for instance, are not considered as foreigners. Thus, what purports to be a self-evident, merely descriptive term turns out to be ideological, reproducing popular stereotypes. It is not possible to analyse the historical roots of *Ausländerfeindlichkeit*, because it does not have any. Jewish people were not foreigners, they were mostly Germans. Nor is it asked how this 'concept of German society' as homogeneous developed, as German citizenship as such has only existed since 1935. The idea of the homogeneous German society derives, in fact, from the Nazi state itself.* (This does not mean, of course, that German nationalism or racism is not much older, but that it had no homogeneous German state on which it could build).

The notion of *Ausländerfeindlichkeit* as hostility also implies that its opposite, friendliness to foreigners, is the correct alternative. But 'friendliness', as in paternalism for instance, can be racist too.

Finally, we want just to touch on a related issue that needs further investigation: one of the main paradigms for conceptualising the presence of immigrants is that of 'cultural identity', a notion which is used from the Left to the Right of the political spectrum. The Right uses it mainly to describe the threat posed by 'foreigners' to German identity. In public political debate, the main fear expressed (sometimes also by liberals) is that of 'foreigners' damaging 'German cultural identity'.

Could it be that this fear stems from Germans' unconscious fear of being reminded of their past? That the identity that is so threatened by the presence of immigrants is that of a non-racist German people? Could this be one reason for their 'hostility', their racism? The singer, Wolf Biermann, who was expelled from the East, and moved to the West, says in one of his songs: 'The Germans have forgiven the Jews but they have not forgiven the Gypsies yet.' And maybe one should add: they are not about to forgive the foreigners either.

Hamburg   ANNITA KALPAKA and NORA RÄTHZEL

---

* See the article by Nora Räthzel in this issue.

Immigrants, migrants and refugees in Europe: a bibliography

Despite Britain's situation as part of the continent of Europe and its membership of the European Community since 1972, material in English on the situation of immigrants and migrants in other European countries is sparse, at least when compared to the vast literature on 'race relations' in Britain itself. This reflects, in part, the insularity of much of British race relations sociology, even in its more radical variants, and the failure of that discipline to engage in an understanding of different European states or in useful comparative work. Now, of course, as Britain moves increasingly close to Europe and as the Single European Market draws nearer, this lack is keenly felt.

This bibliography attempts to bring together the most important and accessible books, pamphlets, reports and journal articles, in English, on the situation of migrant workers, immigrants and refugees in Europe. It is divided into five sections. The first covers material on labour migration which makes specific reference to the European situation. The second lists material on the social, economic and political conditions facing migrants in particular countries. The third section covers fascist and other far-right politics. The fourth section deals with states' policies on immigration and on refugees. The final section lists some of the more useful material on the implications of the Single European Market for migrants, immigrants and refugees.

All the material listed is in English and almost all has been published in Europe, although a few north American sources are included. Most has been published since 1980, although some earlier material has been included to cover gaps or because it remains important. With a few exceptions, general newspaper articles have been excluded.

PAUL GORDON

Migrant labour
Berger, John and Jean Mohr: *A Seventh Man*, Harmondsworth: Penguin, 1975.
Böhning, W.R.: *The migration of workers in the United Kingdom and the European Community*, Oxford: Oxford University Press/Institute of Race Relations, 1972.
—: 'International migration in Western Europe: reflections on the past five years', *International Labour Review*, Vol. 116, no. 4, July-August 1979, pp. 401-14.
—: *Studies in international labour migration*, London: MacMillan: 1984.
Castells, Manuel: 'Immigrant workers and class struggles in advanced

capitalism: the Western European experience', *Politics and Society*, Vol. 5, no. 1, 1975, pp. 33-66.

Castles, Stephen and Godula Kosack: 'The Function of labour migration in Western European capitalism', in Peter Braham (ed.), *Discrimination and disadvantage in employment: the experience of black workers*, London: Harper and Row, 1981.

—: *Immigrant workers and class structure in Western Europe*, Oxford: Oxford University Press, 1985.

Castro-Almeida, Carlos: 'Problems facing second generation migrants in Western Europe', *International Labour Review*, Vol. 116, no. 6, November-December 1979, pp. 763-75.

Cohen, Robin: *The new helots: migrants in the international division of labour*, Aldershot: Gower, 1987.

De Troy, Colette: *The specific training needs of immigrant women: existing and recommended measures to fulfill them*, Brussels: Commission of the European Communities, 1986.

Gorz, André: 'Immigrant labour', *New Left Review*, No. 61, May-June 1970. pp. 28-31.

Grammenos, Stephanos: *Migrant labour in Western Europe*, Maastricht: European Centre for Work and Society, 1982.

Hammar, Tomas: *Democracy and the nation state*, Aldershot: Avebury, 1990.

Hartley, T.C.: *EEC immigration law*, Amsterdam: North Holland, 1978.

Kosack, Godula: 'Migrant women: the move to western Europe – a step towards emancipation?', *Race & Class*, Vol. 17, no. 4, Spring 1976, pp. 369-79.

Lever-Tracey, Constance: 'Immigrant workers and postwar capitalism: in reserve or core troops in the front line?', *Politics and Society*, Vol. 12, no. 2, 1983, pp. 127-57.

Miles, Robert: 'Labour migration, racism and capital accumulation in Western Europe since 1945: an overview', *Capital and Class*, No. 28, Spring 1986, pp. 49-86.

Miles, Robert and Victor Satzewich: 'Migration, racism and "postmodern" capitalism', *Economy and Society*, Vol. 19, no. 3, August 1990, pp. 334-58.

Minet, George: 'Spectators or participants?: immigrants and industrial relations in Western Europe', *International Labour Review*, Vol. 117, no. 1, January-February 1978, pp. 21-35.

Phizacklea, Annie (ed.): *One-way ticket: migration and female labour*, London: Routledge and Kegan Paul, 1983.

Picciotto, Sol: 'The battles of Talbot-Poissy: worker divisions and capital restructuring', *Capital and Class*, No. 23, Summer 1984, pp. 5-17.

Plender, Richard: *International migration law*, Dordrecht: Martinus Nijhoff, 1988.

Rogers, Rosemarie (ed.): *Guests come to stay: the effects of European labour migration on sending and receiving countries*, Boulder, Colorado: Westview Press, 1985.

Salt, John and Hugh Clout: *Migration in post-war Europe: geographical essays*, Oxford: Oxford University Press, 1976.

van Amersfoort, Hans, Philip Muus and Rinus Penninx: 'International migration, the economic crisis and the state: an analysis of Mediterranean migration to Western Europe', *Ethnic and Racial Studies*, Vol. 7, no. 2, April 1984, pp. 238-69.

Social, economic and political conditions

Advisory Commission for Research on Ethnic Minorities: *Ethnic minorities in the Netherlands: a selected list of scientific publications written in English*, Leiden: Advisory Commission for Research on Ethnic Minorities, 1989.

Aronowitz, Alexis: 'Acculturation and delinquency among second-generation Turkish youths in Berlin', *Migration*, No. 4, 1988, pp. 5-36.

Berman, Russell A., Azade Seyhan and Arlene Akiko Teraoko (eds): *New German Critique: Special Issue on Minorities in German Culture*, No. 46, Winter 1989.

Blanc, Maurice: 'Immigrant housing in France: from hovel to hostel to low cost flats', *New Community*, Vol. 11, no. 3, Spring 1984, pp. 225-33.

Booth, Heather: *Guestworkers or immigrants?: a demographic analysis of the status of migrants in West Germany*, Coventry: Centre for Research in Ethnic Relations, 1985.

—: *Second-generation migrants in Western Europe: demographic data sources and needs*, Coventry: Centre for Research in Ethnic Relations, 1985.

Brennan, Paul: 'Surinamers in Holland', *New Society*, 6 November 1975, pp. 314-15.

Brock, C. (ed.): *The Caribbean in Europe: aspects of the West Indian experience in Britain, France and the Netherlands*, London: Frank Cass, 1986.

Campaign Against Racism and Fascism: 'Anti-racist struggles in France', *Searchlight*, December 1980, pp. 16-17.

Castles, Stephen: 'The social time bomb: education of an underclass in West Germany', *Race & Class*, Vol. 21, no. 4, Spring 1980, pp. 369-88.

—: 'West German government plans mass repatriation', *Searchlight*, July 1983, pp. 17-18.

—: 'Racism and politics in West Germany', *Race & Class*, Vol. 25, no. 3, Winter 1984, pp. 37-51.

—: 'Guests who stayed: the debate on 'foreigners' policy' in the German Federal Republic', *International Migration Review*, Vol. 19, no. 4, Winter 1985, pp. 517-34.

Castles, Stephen with Heather Booth and Tina Wallace: *Here for good: Western Europe's new ethnic minorities*, London: Pluto Press, 1984.

Commission of the European Communities: *Eurobarometer: racism and xenophobia*, Brussels: Commission of the European Communities, 1989.

Corbett, Anne: 'Racism surfaces in France', *New Society*, 3 November 1983, pp. 210-11.

Council of Europe: *Migrants in Western Europe: present situation and future prospects*, Strasbourg: Council of Europe, 1987.

—: *Community relations and solidarity: interim report on the community relations project*, Strasbourg: Council of Europe, 1989.

Cross, Malcolm: *Migrant workers in European cities: concentration, conflict and social policy*, Birmingham: Research Unit on Ethnic Relations, 1983.

156   *Race & Class*

—: 'Migrant workers in European cities: forms of inequality and strategies for policy', *Migration*, No. 2, 1987, pp. 5-22.

Cross, Malcolm and Han Etzinger (eds.): *Lost illusions: Caribbean minorities in Britain and the Netherlands*, London: Routledge, 1988.

DeLey, Margo: 'French immigration policy since May 1981', *International Migration Review*, Vol. 17, no. 2, Summer 1983, pp. 196-211.

Domingo, Vernon A.: 'Is there group development after migration?: the case of Surinamers in the Netherlands', *New Community*, Vol. 10, no. 1, Summer 1982, pp. 95-106.

Edye, David: *Immigrant labour and government policy: the cases of the Federal Republic of Germany and France*, Aldershot: Gower, 1987.

Etzinger, Han: 'Immigrant minorities in the Netherlands: research and policy development', *New Community*, Vol. 9, no. 1, Spring-Summer 1981, pp. 84-90.

Freeman, Gary P.: *Immigrant labour and racial conflict in industrial societies: the French and British experience, 1945-1975*, Princeton: Princeton University Press, 1979.

Grillo, R.D.: *Ideologies and institutions in urban France: the representation of immigrants*, Cambridge: Cambridge University Press, 1985.

Guyot, Jean et al.: *Migrant women speak*, London and Geneva: Search Press and World Council of Churches, 1978.

Howe, Darcus: 'Black workers break the French mould', *Race Today*, April/May 1984, pp. 9-15.

Hurtado, Maria Elena: 'Europe's new racism', *South*, November 1986, pp. 17-23.

International Labour Reports: 'Migrant workers in western Europe', *International Labour Reports*, January-February 1985, pp. 15-20.

Joint Council for the Welfare of Immigrants: *Unequal migrants: the European Community's unequal treatment of migrants and refugees*, Coventry: Centre for Research in Ethnic Relations, 1989.

Kornalijnslijper, Nora and Wasif Shahid: 'Immigrants and housing in the Netherlands', *New Community*, Vol. 13, no. 3, Spring 1987, pp. 421-30.

Layton-Henry, Zig (ed.): *Immigration and Politics* (Special issue of *European Journal of Political Research*, Vol. 16, no. 6, November 1988, pp. 587-729).

—: *The political rights of migrant workers in Western Europe*, London: Sage, 1990.

Lloyd, Cathie: 'Immigrant workers in France: trapped in a racist backlash', *International Labour Reports*, January-February 1985, pp. 17-18.

Marin, Yvette: 'Paris under siege', *New Society*, 10 October 1986, pp. 14-16.

Messina, Antony: 'Anti-immigrant illiberalism and the "new" ethnic and racial minorities of western Europe', *Patterns of Prejudice*, Vol. 23, no. 3, 1989, pp. 17-31.

Netherlands Institute of Human Rights and International Alert: *New expressions of racism: growing areas of conflict in Europe*, Studie-en Informationcentrum Mensenrechten No. 7, 1988.

Nielsen, John: 'Racism on the rise', *Time*, 12 December 1983, pp. 8-14.

Oriol, Michel: *Report on studies of the human and cultural aspects of migrations in Western Europe 1918-1979*, Strasbourg: European Science

Foundation, 1980.

Perotti, A.: *Report on 'The fact that aliens belong to various cultures and the tensions which this creates'*, Strasbourg: Council of Europe, 1983.

Plender, Richard: *Introductory report on 'Human rights of aliens in Europe'*, Strasbourg: Council of Europe, 1983.

—: 'Rights of passage', *New Society*, 22 March 1984, pp. 437-39.

—: *Migrant workers in Western Europe*, London: Centre for Contemporary Studies, 1985.

Power, Jonathan: *Migrant workers in Western Europe and the US*, London: Pergamon Press, 1979.

Power, Jonathan and Anna Hardman: *Western Europe's migrant workers*, London: Minority Rights Group, 1984.

Rath, Jan: 'Political participation of ethnic minorities in the Netherlands', *International Migration Review*, Vol. 17, no. 3, Fall 1983, pp. 445-69.

Rex, John, Daniele Joly and Czarina Wilpert (eds): *Immigrant Associations in Europe*, Aldershot: Gower, 1987.

Rist, Ray: 'Guestworkers in Germany: public policies as the legitimation of marginality', *Ethnic and Racial Studies*, Vol. 2, no. 4, October 1979, pp. 402-15.

Runnymede Trust: *Combating racism in Europe: a summary of alternative approaches to the problem of protection against racism and xenophobia in member states of the European Communities*, London: Runnymede Trust, 1987.

Schmitter, Barbara: 'Trade unions and immigration politics in Western Germany and Switzerland', *Politics and Society*, Vol. 10, no. 3, 1981, pp. 318-34.

—: 'Immigrant minorities in West Germany: some theoretical concerns', *Ethnic and Racial Studies*, Vol. 6, no. 3, July 1983, pp. 308-19.

Shahid, Wasif: 'Moroccans in the Netherlands', *New Community*, Vol. 9, no. 2, Autumn 1981, pp. 247-55.

Solomos, John and John Rex (eds): *Migrant workers in metropolitan cities*, Strasbourg: European Science Foundation, 1982.

Sullivan, Scott: 'Uninvited guests', *Newsweek*, 5 February 1990, pp. 18-31.

Thomas, Eric-Jean (ed.): *Immigrant workers in Europe: their legal status*, Paris: UNESCO, 1982.

van Amersfoort, Hans: 'Immigration and settlement in the Netherlands', *New Community*, Vol. 11, no. 3, Spring 1984, pp. 214-24.

van Amersfoort, Hans and Boudewijn Surie: 'Reluctant hosts: immigration into Dutch society 1970-85', *Ethnic and Racial Studies*, Vol. 10, no. 2, April 1987, pp. 169-85.

Veraart, Jan: 'Turkish coffeehouses in the Netherlands', *Migration*, No. 3, 1988, pp. 97-114.

Walraff, Günter: *Lowest of the Low*, London: Methuen, 1988.

Wilpert, Czarina (ed): *Entering the working world: following the descendants of Europe's immigrant labour force*, Aldershot: Gower, 1988.

Wilpert, Czarina: 'From guestworkers to immigrants – migrant workers and their families in the Federal Republic of Germany', *New Community*, Vol. 11, nos. 1/2, Autumn/winter 1983, pp. 137-42.

Zanker, Alfred et al: 'Europe's immigration battles', *US News and World reports*, 31 March 1986, pp. 25-27.

The far right
Aronsfeld, CC: *The Anti Foreigner Campaign in Germany*, London: Institute of Jewish Affairs, 1983.
Backes, Uwe: 'The West German Republikaner: profile of a nationalist populist party of protest', *Patterns of Prejudice*, Vol. 24, no. 1, Summer 1990, pp. 3-18.
Barnes, Ian R: 'The pedigree of GRECE', *Patterns of Prejudice*, Vol. 14, no. 3, July 1980, pp. 14-24 and Vol. 14, no. 4, October 1980, pp. 29-39.
—: 'Intellectual processes on the French far Right', *Patterns of Prejudice*, Vol. 16, no. 1, January 1982, pp. 3-12.
Evrigenis, George (rapporteur): *Report on the findings of the Committee of Inquiry into the Rise of Racism and Fascism in Europe*, Strasbourg: European Parliament, 1986. 169pp.
Ford, Glyn (rapporteur): *Report on the findings of the Committee of Inquiry into Racism and Xenophobia*, Strasbourg, European Parliament, 1990.
Gress, Franz: 'The new right in France and the Federal Republic of Germany' in Nicholas Deakin et al: *The New Right: image and reality*, London: Runnymede Trust, 1986.
Gutman, Nelly: *The reaction against immigrants in France*, London: Institute of Jewish Affairs, 1984.
Harris, Geoffrey: *The dark side of Europe: the extreme right today*, Edinburgh: Edinburgh University Press, 1990.
Hill, Ray with Andrew Bell: *The other face of terror: inside Europe's neo-nazi network*, London: Grafton Books, 1988.
Husbands, Christopher: 'Contemporary right-wing extremism in western European democracies: a review article', *European Journal of Political Research*, Vol. 9, no. 1, 1981, pp. 75-99.
—: 'The dynamics of racial exclusion and expulsion: racist politics in Western Europe', *European Journal of Political Research*, Vol. 16, no. 6, 1988, pp. 701-20.
Johnson, Douglas: 'The new right in France', *New Society*, 12 June 1980, pp. 206-8.
Ó Maoláin, Ciarán: *The Radical Right: a world directory*, London: Longman, 1987.
Plenel, Edwy and Alain Rollat: 'The revival of the Far Right in France', *Patterns of Prejudice*, Vol. 18, no. 2, April 1984, pp. 20-27.
Policar, Alain: 'Racism and its mirror image', *Telos*, No. 83, Spring 1990, pp. 99-100.
Shields, James G: 'Jean-Marie Le Pen and the New Radical Right in France', *Patterns of Prejudice*, Vol. 20, no. 1, January 1986, pp. 3-10.
Taguieff, Pierre-Andre: 'The new cultural racism in France', *Telos*, No. 83, Spring 1990, pp. 109-22.
von Beyme, Klaus (ed.): *Right-wing extremism in Western Europe*, London: Frank Cass, 1988.
Wilkinson, Paul: *The new fascists*, London: Grant McIntyre, 1981.

Immigration and refugee policy
Arnott, Hilary: 'Fortress Europe', *Poverty*, No. 75, Spring 1990, pp. 15-17.
British Refugee Council: *Refugee Manifesto*, London: British Refugee Council, 1989.
Commission of the European Communities: *Comparative survey of conditions and procedures for admission of third country workers for employment in the member states*, Brussels: Commission of the European Communities, 1984.
Convention determining the state responsible for examining applications for asylum lodged in one of the member states of the European Community (1990).
European Consultation on Refugees and Exiles: *A refugee policy for Europe*, London: ECRE, 1987.
Hammar, Tomas (ed.): *European Immigration Policy: a comprehensive study*, Cambridge: Cambridge University Press, 1985.
Joly, Daniele and Robin Cohen (eds): *Reluctant hosts: Europe and its refugees*, Aldershot: Avebury, 1989.
Loescher, Gil: 'The European Community and refugees', *International Affairs*, Autumn 1989, pp. 617-36.
Madureira, Joao: *Aliens' admission to and departure from national territory: case law of the organs of the European Convention of Human Rights and European Social Charter*, Strasbourg: Council of Europe, 1989.
Refugee Forum and Migrants Rights Action Network: *Migrant and Refugee European Manifesto 1989*, London: Refugee Forum, 1989.
Rudge, Philip: 'Fortress Europe', *World Refugee Survey 1986*, pp.5-12.
Seche, Jean-Claude: *Freedom of movement in the community: entry and residence*, Brussels: Commission of the European Communities, 1989.
Vetter, Heinz: *Report on the right of asylum*, Brussels: European Parliament, 1987.

1992 and the Single European Market
Ahluwalia, Amarjit and Sarah Palmer: *1992 – implications for race equality work in local authorities*, London: Local Authorities Race Relations Information Exchange, 1990.
Alibhai, Yasmin: 'Community whitewash', *Guardian*, 23 January 1989.
Böhning, W.R. and J. Werquin: *The future status of third-country nationals in the European Community*, Brussels: Churches Committee for Migrants in Europe, 1990.
Buchan, David and John Wyles: 'The intolerance threshold nears', *Financial Times*, 12 March 1990.
Cohen, Steve: *Imagine there's no countries: 1992 and international immigration controls against migrants, immigrants and refugees*, Manchester: Greater Manchester Immigration Aid Unit, 1990.
Commission for Racial Equality: *Race equality, Europe and 1992*, London: Commission for Racial equality, 1990.
Commission of the European Communities: *Completing the internal market: white paper from the Commission to the Council, Milan, 28-29 June 1985* (COM(85)), Brussels: Commission of the European Communities, 1985.
—: *Communication of the Commission on the Abolition of Controls of Persons*

at Intra-Community Borders (COM (88) 640), Brussels: Commission of the European Communities, 1988.

Cruz, Antonio: *An insight into Schengen, Trevi and other European inter-governmental bodies*, Brussels: Churches Committee for Migrants in Europe, 1950.

Edye, Dave: *1992 and the free movement of labour*, London: European Documentation Centre, Polytechnic of North London, 1990.

Gordon, Paul: *Fortress Europe?: the meaning of 1992*, London: Runnymede Trust, 1989.

—: *1992, the Single European Market and racial equality: a bibliography*, London: Runnymede Trust, 1990.

Home Affairs Committee: *Passport control: report and evidence* (HC 247), London: Her Majesty's Stationery Office, 1987.

—: *Practical police co-operation in the European Community: report and evidence* (HC 363), London: Her Majesty's Stationery Office, 1990.

Jenkins, Jolyon: 'Foreign exchange', *New Statesman and Society*, 28 July 1989, pp. 12-13.

Johal, Jagwant S (ed.): *1992 and the black community: a campaigning report*, Leeds: KAAMYABI, 1989.

Labour Research Department: 'Forgotten workers must be remembered', *Labour Research*, February 1989, pp. 17-18.

—: '1992 and immigration', *Labour Research*, April 1990, pp. 15-17.

Moodley, Ronnie: 'Against Fortress Europe', *International Labour Reports*, No. 38, March-April 1990, pp. 7-11.

Select Committee on European Legislation: *Controls of persons at intra-community borders* (HC 15, part 11), London: Her Majesty's Stationery Office, 1989.

Select Committee on the European Communities: *1992: border control of people – report and evidence* (HL 90), London: Her Majesty's Stationery Office, 1989.

Sivanandan, A.: 'The new racism', *New Statesman and Society*, 4 November 1988, pp. 8-9.

—: 'Racism 1992', *Race & Class*, Vol. 30, no. 3, January-March 1989, pp. 85-90.

Spencer, Michael: *1992 and all that: civil liberties in the balance*, London: Civil Liberties Trust, 1990.

Trades Union Congress: *1992: immigration, freedom of movement and racial equality in Europe: a reading list compiled by the TUC library*, London: Trades Union Congress, 1990.

Webber, Frances: 'Europe 1992', *Race & Class*, Vol. 31, no. 2, October-December 1989, pp. 78-81.

Whose Europe?: racist fortress or equal community, London: Whose Europe, 1989.

Wrench, John: 'Employment and the labour market', *New Community*, Vol. 16, no. 2, January 1990, pp. 275-89.

Racism and the press in Thatcher's Britain

Anti-racists and other demons: the press and ideology in Thatcher's Britain
Nancy Murray

Your daily dose: racism and the Sun
Chris Searle

'Witty, astringent, meticulously researched and engagingly written, these articles expose the popular press' hatchet jobs on the left in general and anti-racism in particular.'
David Edgar (Playwright)

Race & Class pamphlet No. 12
Price: £1.50 (+ 30p p&p)
From: Institute of Race Relations, 2/6 Leeke Street, London WC1X 9HS

Asian and Afro-Caribbean struggles in Britain

A. Sivanandan

From Resistance to Rebellion

£1

Now available in pamphlet form, A. Sivanandan's path-breaking history of black struggle in Britain.

Race & Class pamphlet No.10
£1.00 (+ 25p P&P)

From:
Institute of Race Relations
2-6 Leeke Street
London WC1X 9HS

Institute of Race Relations
EDUCATION SERIES

Roots of racism

Book one in this series covers Europe's early history – the factors that fuelled the original drive for conquest, the dominance of Spanish and Portuguese colonialism, the establishment of the colonial system, and how that fed into Europe's development – in particular, through the Industrial Revolution – slavery and the genesis of racism.

32pp, A4, ISBN 0 85001 023 3. Includes maps, charts, pictures, further reading and suggestions for work. £2.00 + 30p p&p.

Patterns of racism

Book two in this series deals with the different patterns of development of racism and colonialism in different parts of the world to the 20th century. It covers North America, Australia and New Zealand, Southern Africa, Latin America, the West Indies and India. It concludes by looking at the racialist culture that was fostered by imperialism.

48pp, A4, ISBN 0 85001 024 1. Includes maps, charts, pictures, further reading and suggestions for work. £2.50 + 40p p&p.

How racism came to Britain

Book three in this series, using a cartoon format, examines the origins of British racism (in slavery and colonialism) and shows how racism came to dominate every aspect of black life in Britain. Racism in employment, housing, education, the media, the police force, immigration law, the political system are all analysed and graphically illustrated.

44pp, A4, ISBN 0 85001 029 2. Includes suggestions for further reading. £2.95 + 45p p&p.

The fight against racism
A pictorial history of Asians and Afro-Caribbeans in Britain

Book four in this series tells the story of how black people have made history in Britain. Drawing on leaflets, posters, news-sheets and pamphlets from black organisations, as well as over 130 photographs, *The fight against racism* shows how black people have resisted and organised against racism, creating at different times and in different areas new forms and traditions of struggle, from the Second World War to the present day.

48pp, A4, ISBN 0 85001 031 4. Includes suggestions for further reading. £3.50 + 45p p&p.

Orders to the Institute of Race Relations, 2-6 Leeke Street, London WC1X 9HS. Please send cash with order (cheques made payable to **The Institute of Race Relations**). For orders of 10 or more copies there is a 10 per cent discount.